The Campaigns of Napoleon Bonaparte of 1796-1797

Unification of Italy

The Campaigns of
Napoleon Bonaparte
of 1796-1797
Against Austria and Sardinia in Italy

Gustav Joseph Fiebeger

LEONAUR

The Campaigns of Napoleon Bonaparte of 1796-1797
Against Austria and Sardinia in Italy
by Gustav Joseph Fiebeger

First published under the title
The Campaigns of Napoleon Bonaparte of 1796-1797

Leonaur is an imprint
of Oakpast Ltd

ISBN: 978-0-85706-224-6(hardcover)
ISBN: 978-0-85706-223-9 (softcover)

http://www.leonaur.com

Publisher's Notes

In the interests of authenticity, the spellings, grammar and place names
used have been retained from the original editions.

The opinions of the authors represent a view of events in which he
was a participant related from his own perspective,
as such the text is relevant as an historical document.

The views expressed in this book are not necessarily
those of the publisher.

Contents

NAPOLEON BONAPARTE

Napoleon Bonaparte

Born at Ajaccio, island of Corsica, August 15th, 1768; died on the island of Saint Helena, off the coast of Africa, May 5th, 1821. Student in military schools April 23rd, 1779 to 1785; second lieutenant 1785 to 1791; first lieutenant 1791 to 1792; general of brigade 1793; general of division and army commander 1795; consul and first consul 1799; first consul for life 1802; emperor 1804; abdicated 1814; reascended throne and abdicated 1815.

He entered the military school of Brienne, France, April 23rd, 1779, from which he passed to the military school of Paris, October 8th, 1783. Was graduated and assigned to the Artillery, September 1st, 1785. Entered artillery school of Valence, October, 1785, and remained until August 12th, 1786. Served with his regiment of La Fere, at Lyons and Douai until January, 1787, when he went to Corsica on leave. Returned to France and joined his regiment at Auxonne, May, 1788. In September, 1789, he returned to Corsica on leave. Rejoined his regiment at Auxonne, June, 1790, and remained with it until April, 1791, when he was, as first lieutenant, assigned to the artillery regiment of Grenoble, stationed at Valence. In October, 1791, he again visited Corsica on leave. Here he became adjutant and later lieutenant colonel of a volunteer battalion, but still held his rank in the regular army in which he became junior captain January 14th, 1792, and senior captain March 8th, 1793.

He remained in Corsica until June, 1793, when he rejoined his regiment, then belonging to the Army of Italy, at Nice. Upon the revolt at Toulon, he went to Paris, asked for, and received from the Committee of Public Safety, the provisional command of the artillery of the besieging army, which he assumed September, 1793. On November 21st, he became by seniority, the junior major of his regiment, but after the fall of Toulon the representatives of the government with the army nominated him brigadier general, for his valuable services in the siege. He was confirmed January 7th, 1794.

He was assigned as Chief of Artillery of the Army of Italy, and the coast batteries from the Rhone to the Var. He remained with the Army of Italy until April, 1795, and planned operations by which that army advanced by successive steps from Nice to Savona. He went on leave in April, and during a reorganization of the army was placed on waiting orders. Having declined a brigade in the Army of the West he was, in September, 1795, attached to the War Department and assigned to that branch of the topographic department, which had charge of the preparation of plans of campaigns for the armies of the Alps and of Italy.

While on this duty, on October 5th, he was selected by General Barras as his second in command of the Army of the Interior to defend the central government against the attacks of the sections of Paris. His dispositions for meeting the attack were so skilful that the sections were easily repulsed. When Barras gave up the command of the Army of the Interior to become a member of the Directory, General Bonaparte was made general of division Oct. 20, 1795, and appointed commander in chief of that army.

On February 23rd he was assigned to the command of the Army of Italy because of his service to the government in Paris, and because of the great strategic ability displayed in the memoirs he had prepared for the operations of the armies of the Alps and Italy.

The principal campaigns planned and directed by him in person were:

1. **The campaign from April, 1796, to April, 1797**, against first, the Austrian and Sardinian armies later, against the Austrian army. The principal battles of this campaign were those of Montenotte, Dego, Millesimo, Mondovi, Lodi, Lonato, Castiglione, Bassano, Arcole and Rivoli,

2. **The campaign in Egypt from May, 1798**, when he sailed with a corps of 30,000 men from Toulon, until October, 1799, when he returned to France with a few of his principal generals. He landed at Alexandria, occupied Cairo and, with a division of 12,000, marched into Syria as far as Acre. He was unsuccessful in the siege of that town because his siege artillery sent by sea, was captured by the British fleet.

3. **The campaign of 1800, against the Austrians**, in which he

personally directed the operations of the Reserve Army. He crossed the Alps over the Great St. Bernard pass in May, and in June defeated General Melas, in the decisive battle of Marengo. After this he turned over the command of the army to Massena.

4. **The campaign from, August to December, 1805, against the Austrians and Russians**; in this he commanded the Grand Army, organized in 1803 and 1804. He crossed the Rhine toward the end of September and a month later forced the surrender of the Austrian army, under General Mack, at Ulm. He then moved through Vienna into Moravia and defeated the combined Austro-Russian army in the decisive battle of Austerlitz, December 2nd.

5. **The campaign of 1806 against the Prussians.** The Grand Army, which had been encamped in the South German states, was concentrated in northern Bavaria about the 1st of October and on the 14th decisively defeated the Prussians in the battles of Jena and Auerstaedt. Napoleon commanded in the former, and Davout in the latter. He then moved rapidly on Berlin and cut off the retreat of all the Prussians, west of the Oder river.

6. **The campaign of 1806-1807 against the Russians.** After the destruction of the Prussian army, he advanced to the Vistula to seek the Russians. In the vicinity of Warsaw he fought the indecisive battles of Pultusk and Golymin, about the last of December, 1806. The war was then transferred to East Prussia, where he fought the indecisive battle of Eylau in February, 1807. Finally, in June, 1807, he defeated the Russian general, Benningsen in the decisive battle of Friedland.

The war in Spain and Portugal, which followed, lasted from November, 1807, when Marshal Junot marched across the mountains to Lisbon, until the spring of 1814 when Wellington crossed the frontier near Bayonne, about the time Paris was captured by the allies. In this war, which absorbed a large part of the Grand Army, Napoleon was in the field but a short time, from November, 1808, to January, 1809. His operations were successful, but not decisive. During the remainder of the time the operations were conducted by his principal marshals, Massena, Marmont, Ney and Soult.

7. **The campaign of 1809 against Austria.** He defeated Archduke Charles at Eckmuhl near Ratisbon in April, captured that town and then moved along the south bank of the Danube to Vienna. In this vicinity he forced a crossing at the island of Lobau and fought the Battle of Aspen, or Essling, May 22nd. Too weak to advance, he retired

to his island, and awaited reinforcements. In July he again crossed in face of the enemy and won the decisive Battle of Wagram, followed by that of Znaim.

8. The campaign of 1812 against Russia. For this campaign, he assembled an army of 450,000 men, of whom about one-half were French, and the remainder contingents from Austria, Prussia, Saxony, Italy and the smaller German states. His front of operations, at the beginning of hostilities, extended from Riga on the north to Galicia on the south, a distance of 400 miles. At the termination of his advance movement, his centre had advanced to Moscow, 600 miles from the Prussian frontier. He crossed the Nieman River with his main body in the vicinity of Kovno, June 24th, and reached Moscow on September 15th, successfully, but not decisively, defeating the Russians at Smolensk and at Borodino, His army was now scattered over an immense territory; about 90,000 were at Moscow; 30,000 Prussians near the mouth of the Dwina River; 50,000 Austrians and Saxons in Poland and the remainder of his army between these corps and Moscow, His whole army had been largely diminished in strength by the difficulty of supplying it in a country, which was sparsely inhabited and traversed only by very poor roads.

After remaining in Moscow a month, he was obliged to retreat before the winter weather rendered the roads absolutely impassable. The famous retreat began about the 20th of October, and early in November severe winter weather set in. Without provisions or suitable clothing, harassed by the Russians, and suffering from the inclement weather, the army was rapidly transformed into a mob of fugitives without formation or discipline. As the horses were the first to suffer from the famine, the troopers soon joined their companions on foot and the gunners abandoned their pieces. When the army at last reached the Nieman, there was only a rear guard of about 5,000 men, over half of whom were officers, under arms to check the pursuit. The Russians had, however, suffered nearly as much as the French from the weather and lack of supplies and were in no condition to pursue farther.

9. The campaign of 1813 against the allies. As a result of 1812, the Prussians allied themselves with the Russians, who invaded East Prussia, while the remnant of the French army gathered its detachments in Germany and retired to Magdeburg. Napoleon raised a new army in France and marched through south Germany to Dresden winning *en route* the battles of Weissenfels and Gros Gorschen. In the spring the allied army had approached the Elbe, but was forced by Napoleon to the Oder after its defeat at Bautzen; an armistice followed. In August, when hostilities were renewed, Austria and Sweden joined the allies. In September Napoleon defeated the allies in the indecisive Battle of Dresden, but was himself decisively defeated by the allies in October at Leipsic and compelled to fall back to the Rhine. In this campaign he was much embarrassed by the action of his Saxon and other allies, who deserted him at critical moments.

10. **The campaign of 1814, for the defence of France.** About the 1st of January the allies were moving upon Paris with three armies. The southern army moved from Belfort and Strasburg; the central one from the vicinity of Metz and the northern one through Holland. The left and centre were the main armies and were to unite along the line Chalons-Troyes and together advance on Paris. These armies numbered together about 200,000, that in Holland 60,000, while Napoleon had but 100,000 all told. By manoeuvring in the space between the Aisne and Seine Rivers, between Paris and Chalons, he succeeded in separating and checking the centre and left columns of the allies until reinforced by the right. His thin line was finally broken and Paris capitulated March 29th. A week later he abdicated. The principal battles of this campaign were Brienne, Rothiere, Champaubert, Montmirail, Vauchamps, Etoges, Mormont, Montereau, Craonne, Laon, Champenoise, and Montmartre,

11. **The campaign of 1815 in Belgium.** Napoleon returned from Elba March 20th, 1815, and by June had organized an army of 200,000 men. The allies organized an army of 220,000 men in Belgium; of whom 100,000 were commanded by Wellington and the remainder by Blucher; 150,000 on the middle Rhine; 230,000 on the upper Rhine; and 60,000 on the Sardinian frontier. Napoleon concentrated an army of 120,000 in north-eastern France to operate against Wellington and Blucher, and divided his other forces into small corps to act defensively against the heads of the other columns. About the beginning of June he marched against Wellington and Blucher, who were separated, to get in between them and defeat them in detail. He was at first successful at Quartre Bras and Ligny and compelled them to retreat on what he believed were divergent lines.

He pursued Wellington with his main body and found him in a strong defensive position at Waterloo, He attacked him, and had gained

11

but little success, when the approach of the Prussians on his flank turned what might have been an indecisive battle into a decisive defeat and rout. Unknown to Napoleon, Blucher had retreated along a line which led towards Waterloo and was thus able to assist Wellington, while the force sent by Napoleon in pursuit of Blucher, never reached the field. This battle ended Napoleon's military career.

Napoleon abdicated a second time June 21st and shortly thereafter surrendered to the British fleet. He was sent by the British to Saint Helena, where he died.

Until he became emperor. May, 1804, he was known as and signed himself, Bonaparte; after that he was known as, and signed himself, Napoleon.

Napoleon and Beaulieu

Political Situation,—In 1792, Italy was divided into the kingdom of Sardinia with its provinces of Savoy, Nice, Piedmont and Sardinia; the republics of Genoa and Venice; the duchies of Parma, Modena and Tuscany; the Austrian province of Milan; the Papal states; and the kingdom of Naples.

In 1796, Austria, Sardinia and Naples were at war with France. The dukes of Parma and Modena were under the influence of Austria. Because of the violence of the French Revolution, the rulers of the other states, although not actively hostile to France, were not friendly. In all these states there was a middle class of active French sympathizers.

Topographic Situation,—The Maritime Alps and the Apennine mountain ranges separate the narrow strip of territory along the Mediterranean, called the Riviera, from the basin of the Po River. The two ranges are separated by a saddle on the road from Savona to Cairo whose elevation is only 1,600 feet. All roads and trails crossing the Apennines from Savona, Voltri and Genoa reach an elevation of 2,500 feet. The Maritime Alps increase in elevation from Savona westward and at Col de Tenda the road crossing the mountains reaches an elevation of 6,000 feet.

The Riviera about Nice belonged to the kingdom of Sardinia; east of this it belonged to Genoa.

South of the mountains, all the important towns are on the coast and are connected by the road from Nice to Genoa, 125 miles. This road was in bad condition and the French depended largely upon water transportation exposed to capture by the British fleet. This road was later improved by Napoleon and became the famous Corniche road. All the coast towns had small garrisons.

North of the mountains, the Sardinians had the fortified towns of Coni, Mondovi, Ceva, Dego, Acqui, Alessandria, Tortona and Novi.

The shortest road connecting these towns follows the east branch of the Bormida River and near Cairo passes within nine miles of Savona. The principal roads connecting the coast with the Po valley were those connecting Nice and Coni; Oneglia and Albenga with Ceva; Finale and Cairo; Savona and Cairo; Savona and Sassello; Voltri and Novi; Genoa and Novi.

Military Situation.—The war of the French with the first coalition began in 1792. In that year, French troops invaded the Sardinian provinces of Savoy and Nice and these provinces were declared annexed to France. The invading force in Savoy became the Army of the Alps and that in Nice became the Army of Italy.

In June 1793, the Army of Italy attacked the Sardinian army intrenched in the foothills of the Alps between Nice and Tenda and was repulsed. It then retired to the Var and from August to December was engaged in the siege of the insurgent fortified town of Toulon which had opened its harbour to the British fleet. It was here that Napoleon first joined the Army of Italy, as a captain of artillery. It was by following a plan suggested by Napoleon that the town was finally taken; as reward he was promoted to general of brigade in the artillery.

In 1794, the French drove the Sardinians beyond the Col de Tenda and occupied the territory of the republic of Genoa as far east as Savona. This year Napoleon served in the army as chief of artillery and became thoroughly familiar with the mountain passes as far east as Genoa. He also suggested some of the plans to which the success of the French was due.

In April 1795, Napoleon was relieved and placed on waiting orders. In June, the French were driven out of Savona by the Austrians but in November they retook the town and drove the Austrians back over the mountains.

In September, Napoleon was assigned to that bureau of the War Department which dealt with the operations of the field armies; he submitted various memoirs on proposed operations of the Army of Italy and drew up instructions for the army commander. In October, he won the gratitude of the government by dispersing a Paris mob which threatened the national convention.

In March 1796, when Gen. Scherer—the fifth commander of the Army of Italy since its organization—requested to be relieved. Napoleon was appointed to succeed him.

French Army.—When Napoleon took command of the Army of

Italy there were in his territorial department, which extended from Savona in Italy to the mouth of the Rhone River in France, about 60,000 men present for duty and nearly 25,000 sick in the hospitals.

On April 6, he reported his disposable field troops as 45,000 men. This agrees with his returns which show about 43,000 men present in the field army and 2,000 *en route* to join it.

Gen. Laharpe's infantry division of three brigades formed the outpost line covering Savona. One brigade was on the Genoa road at Voltri with an outpost at Pegli. It was sent to this point by the government commissioner with the army who wished to intimidate the Genoese and enable the French to purchase supplies in Genoa. One brigade was guarding the mountain passes on the roads from Savona to Sassello and neighbouring points; this brigade had a strong outpost at Monte Legino and another at Veraggio. One brigade was in the mountains on the road between Savona and Cairo.

Gen. Meynier's infantry division of two brigades was in reserve in the vicinity of Savona.

Gen. Augereau's infantry division of three brigades was at Finale and Loano with strong outposts in the mountains. One brigade was guarding each road and one in reserve.

Gen. Serurier's infantry division of two brigades was at Ormea and Garessio in the Tanaro valley.

These ten brigades had an average strength of 3,600 men or a total of about 36,000 men.

The divisions of Laharpe and Meynier—18,000 men—formed an advance guard under the command of Gen. Massena stationed at Savona.

There were two divisions whose combined strength was but 7,000 men, guarding the Col de Tenda and the passes near the sources of the Var River where the mountains were still covered with snow.

The cavalry of the army—4,500 men—under Gen. Stengel was on its way from southern France where it had spent the winter. It had not all joined.

Napoleon took command at Nice, the department headquarters, March 26, and remained there five days ordering up supplies and troops. On April 5, he was at Albenga where he remained five days more inspecting the troops in the vicinity and organizing his transportation. While here, he learned that the Austrians were advancing through Bochetta Pass and on Sassello and Dego. He made no change in the disposition of his troops, but cautioned his division commanders to be ready to move at a moment's notice, with a full supply of ammunition.

Allied Army.—The allied army opposed to Napoleon was composed of 32,000 Austrians and 17,000 Sardinians. Gen. Beaulieu, who had just arrived from the Rhine, was in command, though he really exercised command only over the left wing composed of the Austrian corps of Generals Argenteau and Sebottendorf—each 14,000 men. The right wing, composed of 17,000 Sardinians and 4,000 Austrians, was under the Austrian general, Colli, who had been attached to the Sardinian army since 1793.

Argenteau's corps had spent the winter near Alessandria, Acqui and Tortona; Sebottendorf's corps at Pavia and other points in the province of Milan. Argenteau had five brigades of infantry; Sebbottendorf, three brigades of infantry and two of cavalry; each infantry brigade numbered about 3,000 men.

Colli's troops extended from Coni to Dego. The greater part of his force was on his right at Coni and Mondovi guarding the direct road from Nice to Turin; two battalions only were at Dego. Provera's Austrian brigade was near Millesimo.

There was also a strong Sardinian force guarding the mountain passes between Piedmont and Savoy, from Lake Geneva to Coni. It was threatened by the Army of the Alps under Kellerman senior.

In a letter to the Directory, April 6, Napoleon estimates the Austrian army as 34,000 infantry and 3,000 cavalry, and the Sardinian army as 45,000. This latter estimate includes the force in front of Kellerman, which Napoleon thought he might be compelled to meet should he advance on Turin.

In numerical strength the two armies actually opposed to each other were approximately equal. The French army had the advantage of position, unless the allies concentrated near Cairo. The French army also had the advantage of a single commander who was familiar with the country and had been for two years studying his problem. The allies had two almost independent commanders, the senior of whom was unfamiliar with the topography of the country and had had no time to make a thorough study of past operations in this territory.

Plans.—The aim of the French government had for some time been to destroy the alliance between Sardinia and Austria. As France was unwilling to restore to Sardinia the provinces of Nice and Savoy, this could only be effected by a decisive victory over the Sardinian troops. Napoleon's predecessor—Gen. Scherer—had been repeatedly directed to attack the Sardinian left flank near Ceva, but in his opinion the condition of the army did not warrant such a movement. It was difficult to subsist the Army of Italy because of its position and the wretched condition of the French system of administration and supply. The army had not been paid and its supply of clothing, arms, ammunition and equipment were very defective. Napoleon had been able to partially remedy some of these defects, but he knew that his only ultimate hope lay in crossing the mountains and living on the enemy's territory. He thoroughly understood the policy of his government and that while Austria was the real enemy to be defeated it was very desirable to detach Sardinia from the alliance.

Beaulieu was directed by his government to confer with Colli and decide on an aggressive campaign.

At a conference between the allied commanders, Colli advocated a concentration at Cairo; but no definite plan was agreed upon. Without informing Colli, Beaulieu later decided to attack the French force at Voltri, by moving two mixed brigades—7,500 men—in two columns from Novi; one *via* Bochetta Pass and the other *via* Campofredda.

At the same time, Argenteau was to move from Acqui on Savona with 8,000 men.

Beaulieu would thus cut off Napoleon's supplies from Genoa and might compel him to evacuate Savona. He assumed that Napoleon would, like most of his predecessors, remain on the defensive as his army could hardly be in a condition to take the field.

Campaign.—As early as April 5, Massena learned of the approach of the Austrians on the roads to Genoa, Voltri, Sassello and Dego. As Napoleon gave him no orders, he strengthened the brigade at Voltri and the post on Monte Legino.

April 10.—On the afternoon of April 10, Beaulieu attacked the French force at Voltri. As the French were expecting him, they made a good defence and with little loss retired that night towards Savona.

Argenteau was expected to attack Monte Legino and the French posts, if any, on the Sassello road, but as his troops were not in position he deferred the attack to the following day.

April 11.—Beaulieu remained at Voltri, April 11, awaiting a report from Argenteau. Argenteau advanced with a force of 3,500 to 4,000 men on the Montenotte road to Monte Legino, sent a brigade on the Sassello road and posted two battalions near Montenotte to protect his communications. He made three unsuccessful assaults on the French force advantageously placed on Monte Legino. This force was originally 1,100 men but was reinforced to 1,500 during the day. That night, Argenteau bivouacked near Montenotte in front of the French works and sent to Dego for two guns as he had no artillery. The Austrian brigade at Sassello was not engaged.

Napoleon was at Savona this day and learned from his *aide*, Marmont—the particulars of the attack at Voltri, and that the French troops had retreated. He also learned from the chief of brigade—Rampon— that the Austrians had made several assaults on Monte Legino and, although repulsed, they still remained in his front. He at once sent Rampon a reinforcement of 700 men and four guns and directed him to hold on until he could be further reinforced.

That night he issued the following orders:—Laharpe with two of his brigades to move on Monte Legino and attack Argenteau in the morning; Massena with Laharpe's third brigade to move along the crest of the mountains to Montenotte and get in Argenteau's rear; Meynier to move with his two brigades to Carcare; Augereau to leave one brigade at Bardinetto to report to Serurier, and with the other two to move on Carcare. Meynier and Augereau were to prevent Colli from sending any troops eastwards; Serurier was directed to keep Colli busy at Ceva without compromising his own troops.

April 12.—Beaulieu, becoming uneasy, started a brigade for Sassello to secure contact with Argenteau. The latter was attacked on the morning of the 12th near Montenotte by Laharpe, defeated, and pursued towards Acqui. The battalions he had posted to cover his line of retreat were defeated by Massena who struck them in succession and they retreated towards Dego. Massena then marched to Cairo.

Napoleon spent the day at Altare on the Savona-Carcare road but established his headquarters at Cairo that night.

April 13.—Beaulieu, informed of Argenteau's defeat, withdrew from Voltri in order to reach Acqui and cover his line of retreat.

Augereau, with Meynier's division and part of his own, attacked Gen. Provera who was on the ridge east of Millesimo with 4,000 men. Provera was defeated and while his main body retreated towards Ceva, Provera himself with about 1,000 men took refuge in the ruined castle of Cossaria, perched on a high hill. Napoleon was with Augereau and directed several unsuccessful assaults on this work. Towards evening he returned to Cairo leaving Augereau to invest the castle.

Massena reconnoitred Dego and Laharpe joined him at Cairo during the day.

April 14.—Augereau called on Provera to surrender, which the latter was compelled to do early in the morning of the 14th, as his men were without food, water or ammunition.

Meynier now reported to Massena at Cairo with one brigade. With Laharpe's division and Meynier's brigade Massena attacked and captured Dego. The Austrians who escaped fled to Acqui; Meynier's brigade was left to hold Dego and Laharpe was ordered to cooperate with Augereau on the 15th.

Knowing that Beaulieu could not assume the offensive with his two Austrian corps. Napoleon decided to capture Ceva if possible.

April 15.—Argenteau's brigade at Sassello had not been engaged but also retired to Acqui. The brigade sent by Beaulieu to Sassello reached there after Argenteau's command had been defeated and the French had gone to Cairo. This brigade moved through Montenotte to Dego and reached there early on the morning of the 15th.

The troops of Meynier's brigade were out of hand on the morning of the 15th being engaged in looting the town. The Austrians without much difficulty retook the town and the French fled to Cairo.

Napoleon at once recalled Laharpe, and in the afternoon of the same day the divisions of Laharpe and Meynier, under the supervision of Massena, recaptured the town. The Austrians fled to Acqui.

Napoleon now became uneasy about Savona in which he had left a small garrison, and ordered Laharpe to march to Sassello the following day to ascertain if any Austrians were marching on Savona.

Massena took temporary command of Meynier's division as the latter was ill.

April 16.—Laharpe went to Sassello while Massena remained near Dego. Augereau attacked Colli at Montezemolo and was repulsed. That night Colli fearing that Serurier, who was advancing, would attack him in rear, retired to the Corsaglia River leaving a garrison in the citadel of Ceva.

April 17.—Laharpe returned to Dego and reported that there were no Austrians in the mountains. Massena was then sent to San Benedetto on the Belbo to guard that flank, while Augereau and Serurier deployed in front of Colli's position on the Corsaglia.

April 18.—Serurier and Augereau made an unsuccessful attack on Colli on the Corsaglia River.

April 19.—Leaving a battalion at Dego, Laharpe moved to San Benedetto while Massena moved into the attacking line in front of Colli. Augereau moved down the river to cross and attack Colli in flank.

Without waiting another attack. Colli fell back to Mondovi.

April 20.—After a desperate battle. Colli was defeated by Massena and Serurier at Mondovi. Augereau remained behind the Corsaglia and Laharpe at San Benedetto.

Armistice of Cherasco.—After the battle of Mondovi, Napoleon moved rapidly to the Stura River to threaten an advance on Turin. On April 23, Colli requested an armistice. Napoleon consented, provided it was preliminary to peace and the fortresses of Coni, Ceva and Tortona were at once surrendered to him.

These conditions being accepted, there was no more fighting between the Sardinians and the French, and on April 28, the armistice was signed and the Sardinians deserted their allies. Besides the three fortresses mentioned the French were to occupy the country limited on the north by the Stura River to Cherasco, the Tanaro River to the Po, and the Po to Parma. They were to use the road *via* Coni, Ceva, Acqui and Tortona as their line of communication through Sardinia under the protection of Sardinian troops.

Until the evacuation of Ceva, Napoleon was worried about his communications which ran through Savona. After the road through Ceva to Ormea was opened, Savona became of small value.

When the campaign closed, Laharpe was at San Benedetto, Augereau at Alba, Massena at Cherasco, Serurier at Fossano and the Col de Tenda brigades were marching on Coni.

It will be observed that on April 21, ten days after Beaulieu's attack on Acqui, Napoleon had solved the first part of his problem by defeating the Sardinians to such an extent that they were willing to desert their allies.

NAPOLEON'S COMMENTS.

1. A French army that occupies the crest of the Apennines covers the Riviera as far as Genoa; but since the army is only two to five leagues distant from the sea, its line can be penetrated in a single day. It would then find itself unable to rally to make its retreat. On account of its little depth, this field of operations is bad and even dangerous.

Had Beaulieu studied the topographic features, he would not have marched on Voltri to cover Genoa, but would have concentrated his army at Acqui and Cairo. From those places he could have advanced in three strong columns of 15,000 each; the left by Montenotte and Savona, the right over the mountains to Finale. The French would have been obliged to fall back from Genoa and Voltri to guard the points attacked. The Austrian general would have operated on ground wholly to his advantage, since he could in a single day cut the French army in two, force it back on the sea and ruin it.

2. After the battle of Montenotte, the Austrians were compelled to rally near Acqui; the Sardinians should at once have moved to Dego to form their right wing. It was an error to assume that to protect Turin it was necessary for them to remain on the direct road to that place. If the two armies had assembled at Dego, they would have thoroughly covered Turin since they would have been on the flank of the road leading to that capital. Had Beaulieu had a few days to rally his troops, it would have been still better to concentrate the armies at Ceva, since then they would have been near the French line of communications. With a strong allied army at Ceva, the French would not have dared to invade Milan. Combined, the two armies were stronger than the French; separated, they were lost.

3. When the French army united to attack Colli, Laharpe was left to watch Beaulieu who was rallying his army at Acqui. Apparently the natural position for this corps was Dego, on the direct line to Savona. Napoleon preferred San Benedetto, farther from Acqui than Dego. From San Benedetto, Laharpe could support the main French army, if necessary, and also take Beaulieu in flank and rear if he decided to advance. It must be observed that at this time the road through Ormea was open to the French and that the road through Savona was not their only line of communications.

4. At Mondovi the divisions of Massena and Serurier only made the attack. This was to leave Augereau on the same side of the Corsaglia River as Laharpe in order to support him should he be attacked by Beaulieu.

Campaign Continued.—After the armistice with the Sardinians, Napoleon placed French garrisons in Coni, Ceva and Mondovi, and prepared to move against Beaulieu before the latter should recover from his defeat.

He reorganized his army and endeavoured to bring it under discipline. As the troops were illy clad, without pay, and on half rations when he took command, he had been rather lenient to infractions in discipline and at Dego and Mondovi suffered partial reverses because of desertions of men from their commands to loot. By requisitions on the conquered country, he now clothed, fed, and paid his army, as well as his defective system of supply would permit, and issued strict orders against looting. This evil was never entirely eradicated.

Gen. Meynier having been assigned to the command of the fortress of Tortona, Gen. Massena assumed permanent command of his division. A new advance guard was organized by forming three battalions of the grenadiers and attaching to them a brigade of four regiments of cavalry. This was commanded by Dallemagne, who had reported from the Col de Tenda division. Gen. Stengel having been killed at Mondovi, Gen. Kilmaine became chief of cavalry. With reinforcements received from Col de Tenda and the soldiers returning to their commands from the hospitals, etc. Napoleon now had a field army of 45,000 men, of whom 5,000 were assigned as garrisons of the Sardinian fortresses.

The Sardinians having withdrawn from the alliance. Gen. Beaulieu retired from Acqui, captured the fortified town of Valenza from his former allies, and crossed to the north bank of the Po. Napoleon had inserted a secret clause in the armistice of Cherasco giving the French the right to cross the Po at Valenza, which was probably communicated to Beaulieu.

Napoleon now decided to cross the Po at Piacenza by surprise. To this end, on May 1, he ordered his advance guard, his cavalry and Laharpe to Tortona *via* Acqui. Augereau and Massena were ordered to follow as soon as the roads were clear. Serurier was to move down the north bank of the Tanaro to a point opposite Valenza, to deceive Beaulieu.

On May 5, the advance guard was near Montebello, the cavalry, Laharpe, Augereau and Massena close behind.

On May 6, active operations began and on the 7th the advance guard, the cavalry, and Laharpe reached the vicinity of Piacenza where, by means of boats and a flying bridge, they crossed the river as rapidly as possible and drove away an Austrian cavalry patrol that was guarding the river bank.

The French at once intrenched themselves on the north bank, and when a force of 5,000 Austrians moved down from Pavia to attack them, they were enabled to defeat the Austrians and drive them in the direction of Pizzighittone. In these operations Gen. Laharpe was accidentally killed by his own men.

Augereau found a ferry above Piacenza that was not guarded and crossed at that point. Massena crossed at Piacenza after Laharpe, but was not on the north bank until the morning of the 9th.

That day the divisions of Massena and Augereau, preceded by the advance guard and cavalry, moved towards Lodi to intercept Beaulieu, who was retreating *via* Pavia and Lodi. Laharpe's division remained in position watching the Austrians at Pizzighittone.

On May 10, the French troops reached Lodi and found that Beaulieu had crossed the Adda to the east bank leaving a battalion in the town. This battalion crossed the river as soon as the French appeared. The wooden bridge, 250 yards long, had not been destroyed; but a rear guard—twelve battalions and fourteen guns—had been left by Beaulieu to defend it. Beaulieu himself had followed the Adda southwards to Cremona.

Napoleon at once established a number of guns on the west bank at Lodi and the greater part of the day was spent in a harm- less artillery duel. Late in the afternoon Napoleon decided to storm the bridge, but first sent his cavalry to cross at a ford higher up.

The storming column, consisting of a battalion of light infantry followed by his grenadiers, formed behind the walls of the town and suddenly advanced out on the bridge. Their advance was soon checked by the Austrian artillery; and, to carry the column forward, Generals Massena, Berthier, Dallemagne, and Chief of Brigade Lannes, placed themselves at the head of the column. When the column was checked a second time, the light infantry leaped into the shallow river and engaged the batteries and Austrian infantry. This enabled the grenadiers to cross the bridge and attack the Austrian rear guard. The Austrians retreated with a loss of about 500 men and a few guns.

The theatrical storming of the bridge at Lodi had a great moral effect both on the French and the Austrian soldiers.

The Austrian troops were pursued by the advance guard and Augereau as far as Crema and Cremona, while the cavalry went northward to ascertain whether any other Austrian troops were retreating to Brescia.

The advance guard and Laharpe's division were then posted along the Adda, and Serurier's division at Piacenza, which it had reached on the 10th. Augereau moved to Pavia and Massena to Milan.

Napoleon entered Milan with Massena on May 16, about a month after the battle of Montenotte. Here he started the siege of the citadel, then held by 2,000 Austrian troops left by Beaulieu, and organized a new government.

On May 20, he learned that peace was finally signed between Sardinia and France and he felt able to again advance, as his communications were secure and he could count on reinforcements from the Army of the Alps.

Augereau was directed to move to Milan, Massena to Lodi, and Serurier to Cremona; the three divisions then moved to Brescia. The cavalry and advance guard preceded the columns; Laharpe's division moved with Massena's central column. Gen. Despinoy, who had been on Napoleon's staff, was assigned to the command of Milan.

Beaulieu, who had retired to the fortress of Mantua, was thus obliged to withdraw his army from the vicinity of that fortress to defend the upper Mincio and protect his communication with the Tyrol in Austria.

From Brescia, Napoleon, with his advance guard, cavalry, Massena and Serurier moved on Valeggio, while Augereau moved on Peschiera. When Kilmaine, who temporarily commanded both the cavalry and advance guard, forced the Mincio on May 30, at Valeggio where it was fordable, Beaulieu retreated to Rivoli and then made his way to Roveredo in the Tyrol. A strong Austrian garrison was left in Mantua.

This closed the campaign of Napoleon and Beaulieu, which had lasted a little less than two months.

NAPOLEON'S COMMENTS.

1. To defend the passage of the Po, Beaulieu took a position near Valenza. This could fulfil his object only when opposing an army that was incapable of manoeuvring. He should have placed himself astride the Po, near Stradella, where he should have constructed two bridges with strong bridgeheads. This would have prevented the French from moving down the south bank of the Po and compelled them to cross it above the bridges. The Austrian general would then have had the advantageous lines of the Po and Ticino as lines of defence.

2. It is said that Napoleon should have crossed the Po at Cremona instead of Piacenza; he would then have turned the Adda as well. This is wrong; his movement was already an audacious one. To have still further extended his army was to tempt the enemy to attack its parts in detail. Furthermore, at Piacenza, which is on the south bank, it was more probable that boats would be found for the crossing than at Cremona, which is on the north side.

3. It is said that Napoleon should have advanced at once after Lodi,

for he would then have found Mantua unprepared for defence. Such a movement would have been hazardous. There were fortified places in rear, and governments to be established in the province abandoned by the Austrians. The French were as active and rapid in their movements as could be expected; more would have been impossible. In the six days the army rested in Lombardy, it doubled its effective power by increasing its artillery, remounting its cavalry, and rallying its stragglers.

4. Instead of attempting to defend the line of the Mincio, which is weak, Beaulieu should either have assembled his whole army in the district south of Mantua and drawn his supplies from the country south of the Po, or he should have assembled it about Gavardo or further north. This would have prevented the French army from crossing the Mincio.

If he felt too weak to do either, he should have assembled it on the plateau of Rivoli without entering Peschiera. The precedent he established in violating the neutrality of Venice by occupying this fortress compelled the Venetians to yield the fortresses of Peschiera, Verona, and Legnago to the French.

FRENCH GENERALS OF DIVISION.

Augereau, Pierre Francois.—Born in Paris 1757. He enlisted in the Neapolitan cavalry and was a sword master in 1792 when he returned to France and entered the volunteers. He rose rapidly and in 1794 was a general of division. In 1804 he was made a marshal of France. He served in the Army of the Pyrenees, in the Army of Italy, 1796-7; commanded the Army of the Rhine-Moselle, 1798; the Army of Holland, 1800, and as commander of the VII. corps took part in the campaigns of Austerlitz, Jena, Eylau and Friedland. Served in Spain in 1809, and under Napoleon in 1812-13-14. He hastened to join the Bourbons in 1814 and his services were declined by Napoleon upon his return from Elba and by the Bourbons on the second restoration. He died in 1816. Under the Empire he was made Duke of Castiglione.

"Strong character, courage, firmness, energy, experience in warfare, liked by his men and is lucky."—Napoleon August 14, 1796.

Berthier, Alexandre.—Born in 1753 and entered the general staff in 1770. Served as chief of staff of several different armies of the revolution before becoming Chief of Staff of the Army of Italy. In 1799 he became minister of war and in 1800 the nominal commander of the Reserve Army. In 1804 he became a marshal of France. He accompanied Napoleon in all his campaigns as chief of staff until his abdication in 1814. He then supported the Bourbons and retired from France during the Hundred Days. He was killed somewhat mysteriously during that period. He was one of the French officers who served under Rochambeau in America. Under the Empire he was made Duke of Valengin, Prince of Wagram and Sovereign Prince of Neuchatel.

"Talent, energy, courage, character. Is ambitious."—Napoleon August 14, 1796.

Dallemagne, Claudius.—Born in 1754. Entered army as volunteer in 1773. General of brigade 1793; general of division 1797; died 1810. Performed distinguished service at Lodi, Lonato, Castiglione, Lavis and Mantua. In 1798 invested the fortress of Ehrenbreitstein on the Rhine and forced its capitulation. Senator in 1806 and commandant of 25th military division in 1809.

Kilmaine, Charles Edward.—Born in Ireland 1751. Entered French service in 1774; adjutant in 1778; captain in 1778; lieut. col. in 1792; colonel in 1793; general of brigade in 1793; general of division in 1794. Died in Paris in 1799. Served in northern armies until 1795; served in Armies of Alps and Italy until 1798, then temporary commander of the Army of England.

"Especially good as commander of a detached body in any operation requiring discretion, ability and calmness."—Napoleon at St. Helena.

Laharpe, Amedee Emmanuel.—Born in Switzerland 1754. Forced to leave his country an account of liberal views, entered French army and became chief of battalion of volunteers 1792; general of brigade for services at Toulon 1793; general of division 1795; was killed accidentally by his own troops at Fombio, Italy, in 1796. From 1793 to 1796 he served in the Army of Italy.

"An officer of distinguished bravery. A grenadier in heart and stature. Beloved by his troops whom he led with intelligence."—Napoleon at St. Helena.

Massena, Andre.—Born in Nice in 1758 and enlisted in the infantry in 1775. In 1789 he left the service, having reached the grade of non-commissioned officer. He entered the volunteers and was elected chief of battalion in 1792. In 1793 he became general of brigade and general of division, and in 1804 marshal of France. His service was with the Army of Italy from 1792 to 1797. In 1798 he commanded the French corps at Rome and in 1799 the Army of Switzerland. In 1800 and again in 1805-6 he commanded the Army of Italy. In the

Friedland campaign he commanded the right wing of the army about Warsaw. He took part in the campaign of 1809 on the Danube and in 1810 was sent to Spain and Portugal where he remained until the summer of 1811. After his unsuccessful campaign in Spain, Napoleon refused to give him a field command. He took service under the Bourbons and took no part in the affairs of the Hundred Days. He lost favour with the Bourbons because he was a member of the court-martial which refused to try Marshal Ney. He died in 1817. Under the Empire he was made Duke of Rivoli and Prince of Essling.

"Active, indefatigable; has boldness, military instinct and promptness in deciding."—Napoleon August 14, 1796.

Serurier, Jean Matthieu.—Born 1742. Entered army 1760, major 1789, general of brigade 1793, general of division 1795, marshal 1804. Served in Hanover 1760, in Poland 1762, in Corsica 1768, in Army of Italy 1792-1799. Governor of Invalides and commandant of National Guard under Consulate and Empire but was not in the field. Did not serve under Louis XVIII., but served during the Hundred Days. Died 1819.

"Fights like a soldier, assumes no responsibility, firm, has a poor opinion of his men."—Napoleon August 14, 1796.

Stengel, Henri.—Bavarian who entered French service in 1762; first lieutenant 1765; captain 1769; major 1788; general of brigade 1792; general of division 1794. Served in the northern armies until 1796. Killed at Mondovi 1796.

"Adroit, intelligent, alert; was a true general of outposts, collecting all military and topographic information without being directed; combined the qualities of youth with the experience of age."—Napoleon at St. Helena.

AUSTRIAN ARMY COMMANDERS.

Beaulieu, Jean Pierre de.—Born in Belgium in 1725 and entered the army in 1743. Served as a company officer in the Seven Years' War, 1756-1763. In 1789 he became a brigade commander in the Austrian army, a division commander in 1790, and served with distinction against the French in Belgium from 1792 to 1795. He retired in 1796 and died in 1819.

Colli-Marchei, Baron Michele Angelo Alessandro.—Born in Piedmont, Italy, 1738, and entered the Austrian service in 1756. He was a company officer until 1768, a field officer until 1787; attained the rank of division commander in 1793. He was in the Sardinian army 1793-

1796, and later served in the Papal and Neapolitan armies. He died in 1808.

AUSTRIAN ARMY—APRIL 1, 1796.

Beaulieu—General in Command.

Wings	Brigades	Battalions	Squadrons	Stations
	Liptay	4	—	Aqui
	Ruccavina	4	—	Cortemiglia
Argenteau	Pittoni	7	—	Alexandria
	Sallich	5	2	Tortona
	Kerpen	5	—	Pavia
Sebottendorf	Schubirz	—	18	Pavia
	Nicoletti	6	—	Lodi
	Roselmini	4	—	Lodi

There were also 13 squadrons of Neapolitan troops serving with Sebottendorf.

Total, 35 battalions, 33 squadrons, 28,000 men.

ARMY OF ITALY—APRIL 4, 1796.

General in Chief, Bonaparte.

Aides de Camp, Murat, Junot, Marmont, Lemarrois, Louis Bonaparte.

Chief of Staff, Berthier, General of Division; Assistant Chief of Staff, Vignolle, Adjutant General; Chief of Artillery, Dujard, General of Division; Chief *Commissaire*, Chauvet.

Generals of Division	Generals of Brigade	Strength
	Pijon	
Laharpe	Menard	11,075
	Cervoni	
Massena.		
	Dommartin	5,428
Meynier	Joubert	
	Beyrand	
Augereau	Victor	7,908
	Banel	
Serurier	Guieu	6,938
	Pelletier	
Macquard	David	3,690
	Dallemagne	
	Davin	

28

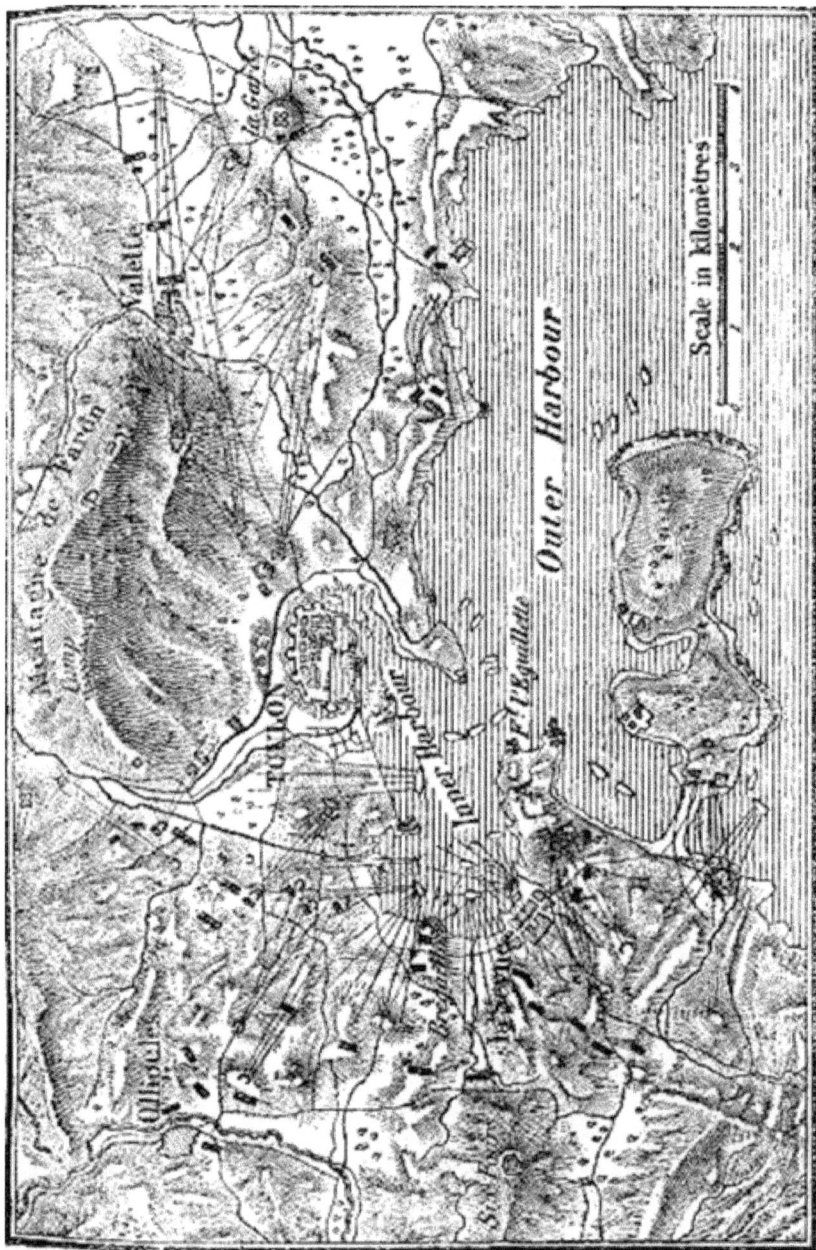

Scale in kilomètres

Outer Harbour

F.t l'Eguillette

Inner Harbour

TULLO_

La Garde

Valette

Montagne de Pharon

Malbousquet

Garnier	Verne	3,136
	Bizanet	
	Colomb	
Stengel	Cavalry	2,542
Kilmaine		2,000

Total present in field army,		42,717
Coast Divisions		21,639

Total present,		64,356
Sick in hospitals		24,427

The organization of the divisions of Augereau and Serurier was somewhat modified before the 11th, since Napoleon mentions Gens. Rusca, Fiorella and Miollis as brigade commanders in these divisions. The best authorities now agree that on the 10th of April Napoleon had in his four leading divisions between 40,000 and 41,000 men, of whom 35,000 were infantry, and of the remainder two-thirds cavalry and one-third artillery.

Napoleon and Wurmser

The Italian Quadrilateral.—The fortresses of Verona and Legnago on the Adige River and those of Peschiera and Mantua on the Mincio River form the Italian Quadrilateral. Legnago and Peschiera were small fortifications designed principally as bridgeheads and not requiring large garrisons. Verona was a large walled town lying on both sides of the Adige and had several detached forts. It was a bridgehead of great value as it covered several bridges, had a citadel, and was capable of strong defence.

Mantua was a large walled town on the west bank of the Mincio but as a fortress it owed its value to its peculiar situation. The Mincio here forms a lake which almost encircles the town and leaves only a small part of the perimeter to be defended. The east bank of the Mincio was connected with the town by two long bridges and causeways. The one running due north from Mantua terminated in a permanent fort—the citadel of Mantua—which formed a strong bridgehead. The other was also covered by a permanent bridgehead. The south-western face of the city was accessible by land but was covered by strong fortifications.

The Adige River between Verona and Legnago is a serious obstacle; being unfordable, very swift and over 400 feet wide. The Mincio although as wide as the Adige is fordable in the summer months and is not a serious obstacle.

The principal east and west roads through the Quadrilateral are the Verona–Peschiera and the Legnago–Mantua roads. On the former, Brescia is thirty and Peschiera seventeen miles west of Verona; Villanova is thirteen and Vicenza is thirty miles east of Verona. On the latter road Cremona is forty and Marcaria thirteen miles west of Mantua; Legnago is thirty and Padua seventy miles east of Mantua.

An Austrian army entering Italy from the north, passes the Alps by Brenner Pass and reaches Trent on the Adige River. An Austrian army entering Italy from the east, passes through the plain between the mountains and the Adriatic and reaches the Brenta River near Cittadella. If armies are moving into Italy by both lines simultaneously they may when they reach the Brenta be concentrated either at Trent or Cittadella and advance on the Quadrilateral by any of the various roads shown on the map.

From Trent to Bassano where the river emerges from the mountains is a distance of sixty miles. Cittadella is ten miles from Bassano, forty-five from Verona, and one hundred from Legnago *via* Padua.

Roads From Trent to the Quadrilateral.—From Trent the principal road is that along the east side of the Adige which follows the bank of the river to Verona—fifty-five miles. This road is most easily blocked at the gorge of the river just below Rivoli and sixteen miles from Verona; the French later constructed a fort at this gorge on the east side of the river. Roveredo is the principal town on this road, being the centre of a network of roads. Between Roveredo and Trent the road and river run through the gorge of Calliano.

All the roads between the Adige and Lake Garda start from the Roveredo-Riva road and unite at the plateau of Rivoli. One follows the west bank of the river to a point above Rivoli where on account of the gorge it ascends the plateau—three or four hundred feet above the river—and runs to Castelnovo. The two others are inferior roads; one along the lake shore and the other in the valley east of Monte Baldo. The latter passes through the defile of Corona.

West of Lake Garda the valley of the Chiese River may be reached by road either from Trent or from Roveredo. The roads unite at Storo. Along Lake Idro there is a single road following a narrow shelf at Rocca d'Anfo. Below Lake Idro one road runs to Brescia which is ninety miles from Trent; one follows the river, passing through Gavardo, with a branch running to Salo on Lake Garda. There was no road between Salo and Riva along the west shore of Lake Garda.

The road from Trent to Lake Idro passes the divide between the Sarca and the Chiese at an elevation of 2,700, feet and that from Riva to Lake Idro over a divide 2,500 feet in elevation. Lake Idro itself has an elevation of 1,600 feet. The mountain ranges inclosing the Adige, Lake Garda and the Chiese all have summits whose elevation exceeds 7,000 feet.

Lake Garda.—Lake Garda is the largest of the lakes of northern

Italy being thirty-four miles long, and eleven miles wide at its broadest part. Sailing vessels on the lake formed the usual means of transport.

First Campaign

Military Situation.—After the retreat of Beauleau, Gen. Sauret reported to Napoleon to replace Gen. Laharpe and was assigned to the command of the troops west of Lake Garda. Gen. Vaubois also reported with a division from the Army of the Alps.

To Massena was assigned the task of covering the besieging forces at Mantua. With Sauret's division of 4,000 men he was to guard the roads west of Lake Garda, and with his own division increased to 15,000 men he was to hold the space between Lake Garda and the Adige River as far south as Ronco. A French garrison was placed in Verona.

The rest of the troops were to drive the Austrians—10,000 men—who were encamped around Mantua across the Mincio into the fortress where they were to be watched by Serurier assisted by Kilmaine while Augereau guarded the Adige above and below Legnago. In order to reduce the citadel and fortress of Mantua, orders were sent to Coni, Nice and other points for siege artillery.

During the month of May, Napoleon had made terms with the Dukes of both Parma and Modena by which they agreed to make large contributions for the support of the army. As it would be some time before the Austrian army could again take the field, he determined to utilize this time in forcing the other powers of Italy to make peace.

On June 5, at Brescia, he signed an agreement with the representatives of the King of Naples. The following day he started *via* Milan for Tortona and from that point arranged matters with Genoa.

While at Tortona he directed Augereau to march with a part of his division on Bologna, and Vaubois to march with his division *via* Modena on Leghorn.

At Bologna, June 23, he came to an agreement with the representatives of the Pope, and on June 27 visited Vaubois at Leghorn to adjust matters in Tuscany. Having received information that a new Austrian army was being assembled in Trent to relieve Mantua, he now hastened back to his army and directed Augereau to recross the Po and return to his position on the Adige.

On June 30, the citadel of Milan surrendered to Gen. Despinoy and he was directed to leave a small garrison under Gen. Sahuguet and join the army with three *demi*-brigades.

On July 6, Napoleon reported to his government that Gen. Wurmser, the new Austrian commander, was at Trent with an army of 49,000 regulars. He gave the strength of his own army as 44,000 men. In round numbers Massena had 15,000; Sauret, 4,500; Augereau, 5,000; Despinoy, 5,500; Kilmaine, 2,000; Serurier, 10,000. About 2,000 of Despinoy's division, not included above, were at Bergamo.

Sauret's troops were at Salo, Gavardo and Desenzano and a small detachment at Brescia. Massena had outposts at Torri, Corona and in the valley of the Adige, a strong reserve at Rivoli, a garrison in Verona, and a *demi*-brigade along the river below the city. Despinoy had one *demi*-brigade on the Adige between Massena and Augereau and another in Peschiera. Augereau occupied Legnago and guarded the river above and below. Kilmaine with the cavalry reserve was near Villafranca.

Napoleon at this time believed the roads west of Lake Garda impracticable for a large force and expected the Austrians to force the gap between the Adige and Lake Garda or attempt to cross that river below Verona.

During the month of July, Napoleon tried unsuccessfully to capture Mantua by surprise, employing boats to take his men across the lake which surrounded the fortress. On July 18, the siege guns having arrived, the first parallel was opened and the chief engineer promised to reduce the place in twenty days. The siege was however interrupted by Gen. Wurmser.

Campaign.—In the latter part of July, Gen. Wurmser moved out from Trent leaving garrisons in the Tyrol.

Wurmser's plan was to attack the French line in three columns. A column of four mixed brigades—18,000 men—under Gen. Quasdanovich, was to move down *via* Lake Idro to attack the French posts west of Lake Garda. A central column of seven brigades—24,000 men—commanded by himself, was to move down the Adige and on each side of Monte Baldo—15,000 west of the Adige River and 9,000 east of that river. A flying column of one brigade of infantry and one brigade of cavalry—5,000 men—under Gen. Meszaros, was to move *via* the Brenta valley and Vicenza to secure Verona and Legnago the minute they were evacuated by the French.

July 29.—Early in the morning of July 29, Wurmser's central column attacked Joubert's brigade of Massena's division at Corona; and, though reinforced, the French outpost line was, during the day, forced back to Rivoli. Sauret was attacked by one brigade at Salo and was compelled to retreat to Desenzano. A second Austrian brigade defeated the French force at Gavardo which fell back to Salo and took refuge in an old castle where it was invested. The other Austrian brigades moved on Brescia.

Napoleon was at Brescia in the morning and hastened to Peschiera. His first orders were for a counter-attack, but this was soon abandoned. Despinoy and Kilmaine were ordered to Castelnovo to support Massena. Augereau was ordered to retreat to Roverbella.

July 30.—On the west side of Lake Garda two Austrian brigades reached Brescia and one Austrian brigade reached the Chiese River at San Marco on the Lonato road. The fourth brigade remained at Salo. Wurmser's column was engaged all day in concentrating at Rivoli and attacking Massena. Meszaros took Verona and Legnago as soon as abandoned by the French. He took no active part in the campaign but protected Wurmser's communications.

Sauret was at Desenzano; Massena was obliged to fall back to Castelnovo; Augereau was on the road between Legnago and Mantua; Despinoy and Kilmaine at Castelnovo.

That night Napoleon definitely decided his plan of action, which was to make his communications safe, by first attacking the Austrians west of Lake Garda. Sauret and Despinoy were to recapture Salo, release the French, and march on Brescia; Massena was to abandon the east bank of the Mincio, leaving a small force to hold Peschiera and the bridge at Valeggio, and send one *demi*-brigade to Augereau; with the remainder of his troops he was to retire to Desenzano; Serurier was to abandon the siege of Mantua and send his troops east of the Mincio to join Augereau; with those west of the Mincio, he was to fall back to Marcaria and hold the crossing; Augereau, reinforced by Kilmaine and by troops from Serurier and Massena, was to march for Brescia and recapture it.

July 31.—Two of the Austrian brigades west of the Mincio moved from Brescia to Montechiaro on the Chiese River; the one at San Marco on the Lonato road advanced to Lonato, where it attacked Despinoy, defeated him, was in turn defeated by Massena and returned to San Marco. The fourth remained at Salo.

Wurmser advanced from Castelnovo to the Mincio and gave orders for the investment of Peschiera. He made no attempt to cross the river or to advance on Mantua.

Sauret made a night march on Salo and relieved the troops that had taken refuge in the old castle. He could not march on Brescia, as Napoleon had ordered, since Despinoy had not accompanied him. He therefore returned to Desenzano. Despinoy was moving to support Sauret, when he was attacked by the Austrians near Lonato.

Massena withdrew to Desenzano and in the afternoon marched to Lonato to assist Despinoy.

Augereau and Kilmaine, under Napoleon, were at Roverbella. They covered Serurier while he was withdrawing his troops from the besieging lines, destroying his works, and dismounting his guns. Serurier with two brigades retired to Marcaria.

August 1.—Quasdanovich, hearing nothing from Wurmser and learning that his brigades had met defeat at Salo and Lonato, ordered his three advance brigades to fall back towards Gavardo. Wurmser, after leaving a besieging force at Peschiera and a strong force at Castelnovo to cover his communications, marched to Mantua.

Augereau and Kilmaine under Napoleon with a column of 12,000 men crossed the Mincio at Goito during the night of July 31- August 1, and moved on Brescia, driving the enemy's detachments from their front. Sauret and Despinoy joined them at the Chiese. The French reached Brescia in the evening of August 1, just as the Austrians were evacuating. In passing Castiglione, Augereau left a brigade at that place to cover his rear.

August 2.—Quasdanovich was assembling three brigades at Gavardo; the fourth again took possession of Salo. Wurmser was at Mantua, completing the destruction of the French besieging works and moving their cannon into the fortress. He sent a reconnoitring force *via* Goito towards Brescia to ascertain the position of Quasdanovich.

Massena remained near Lonato and Sauret returned to that place; Despinoy remained at Brescia where his troops from Bergamo joined him. Augereau and Kilmaine moved back to Montechiaro on the Chiese.

That afternoon Napoleon learned that the French brigade at Castiglione had retreated before Wurmser's reconnoitring force without fighting. Assuming that Wurmser was behind this column he was for a time thoroughly discouraged and inclined to order a general retreat behind the Adda. He recovered from his depression, however, and decided not to retreat.

He therefore ordered Sauret's division to again make a night march from Lonato and retake Salo. Dallemagne, who commanded a brigade under Sauret, was to move on Gavardo and cooperate with Despinoy, who was to march to the same place from Brescia. Augereau and Kilmaine were to advance to Castiglione and hold Wurmser should he advance.

August 3.—Quasdanovich decided to leave a brigade at Gavardo and advance with the others to find Wurmser. En route to Lonato he struck in succession Despinoy and Dallemagne and drove them back. His fourth brigade from Salo reached Lonato *via* Desenzano and its commander surprised one of Massena's brigades and captured part of it. Massena came to the rescue and the Austrian brigade was defeated and almost destroyed. Quasdanovich again withdrew towards Gavardo. Wurmser advanced with a strong force and joined his reconnoitring force at Castiglione, where he had an engagement with Augereau and Kilmaine.

On the morning of the 3rd, Sauret's division returned to Salo, without passing through Desenzano and in turn invested a part of an Austrian fourth brigade. The operations of Despinoy, Dallemagne and Massena have been described. In a brilliant engagement at Castiglione, Augereau and Kilmaine defeated the force that Wurmser had brought to that place.

That night Napoleon directed Massena to reinforce Sauret's division and ordered the Austrian communications to be seriously threatened both from Salo and Brescia.

August 4.—Quasdanovich, having lost one of his brigades and being threatened from Salo and Brescia, was afraid to advance with his whole force but sent a mixed brigade of 2,000 men to find Wurmser. This force almost captured Napoleon when it appeared suddenly at Lonato; its commander, however, being informed that he was in the presence of the whole French army, surrendered his command. When he learned of this loss, Quasdanovich ordered his brigades to fall back to Lake Idro.

Wurmser concentrated his force this day to make a serious attack on Augereau.

That night Napoleon decided that his communications were no longer threatened and that he could attack Wurmser with impunity.

August 5.—The decisive battle of the campaign took place this day at Castiglione, where Wurmser had assembled about 20,000 men.

Napoleon employed in his attack all of his available troops—30,000 men. The division at Salo was the only one absent. The two brigades of Serurier's division at Marcaria marched to the field and attacked the Austrians in flank and rear.

Wurmser fought a stubborn battle but was finally compelled to retreat across the Mincio.

August 6.—Massena, followed by Augereau, marched in haste to reinforce the French garrison of Peschiera—which was about to surrender—and to cross the Mincio in order to cut off Wurmser's retreat. Being warned in time, Wurmser decided that night to leave part of his troops as a garrison in Mantua and with the remainder withdraw to Rivoli and Verona.

August 8 to 10.—Napoleon ordered Sauret to advance *via* Lake Idro, Massena on Rivoli, and Augereau on Verona. By August 10, Sauret was at the junction of the roads north of Lake Idro, Massena at Rivoli and Corona, and Augereau at Verona. Each of the three columns of Wurmser's army retired over the roads on which it advanced. Meszaros stopped at Bassano.

At the close of this two weeks' campaign. Gen. Despinoy was sent to command a fortress in Sardinia and his troops given to Gen. Sauret. Gen. Sauret, who was injured during the campaign, was later replaced by Gen. Vaubois. Gen. Serurier, who was seriously ill, was replaced by Gen. Sahuguet. Gen. Serurier later took the command in Tuscany which had been held by Vaubois.

With the troops left by Wurmser, the Mantua garrison now numbered five brigades—15,000 men.

The French troops were much exhausted by this campaign, and it was not until August 24, that the Austrian garrison at Mantua was attacked and forced to cross to the west side of the Mincio.

As all the siege material and works had been destroyed either by the French or the Austrians, Napoleon was compelled to resort to investment alone. This however was not sufficiently close to cut off all supplies from the south.

NAPOLEON'S COMMENTS.

1. The plan of Marshal Wurmser was defective; his three columns were separated from each other by two rivers, the Adige and the Mincio, by Lake Garda, and by several chains of mountains.

2. Wurmser should have done one of two things:

First:—He might have advanced with his whole force between Lake Garda and the Adige River and taken possession of the plateau of Rivoli. To this point he could have brought his artillery by the river road. Thus posted, with his right on Lake Garda, his left on the Adige, with a front of only three leagues, he would have been too powerful for the French army.

Second:—He might have debouched with his whole army by the Chiese on Brescia; the artillery could have taken this route.

3. In the execution of his plan, he made another mistake, for which he paid dearly; it was in losing two days by going to Mantua. He should have thrown two bridges over the Mincio out of cannon range of Peschiera and promptly crossed this river to join his right column at Lonato, Desenzano, or Salo, and thus rapidly repaired the defects of his plan.

To operate by lines separated from each other is a mistake which usually compels one to commit a second. The detached column has orders only for the first day; its operations for the second day depend on what happens to the main column. It therefore either loses time in awaiting further orders or it operates by chance.

It is then a principle that an army should always have its columns so united that an enemy cannot get in between them.

4. The division of Sauret should have had an advance guard at Rocca d'Anfo on Lake Idro to reconnoitre the country to the north; this would have prevented the surprise of Salo and Brescia. These places would then have had twelve hours warning and could have been prepared for defence.

5. Since there is west of Lake Garda but a single practicable road for artillery which passes through Rocca d'Anfo, an army must pass this defile to reach Salo. Would it not have been better to post Sauret at this point and occupy by redoubts, intrenchments, and two armed boats the roads and the lake? It would have taken the Austrian right column twenty-four hours to take this place, and Brescia, Salo, and army headquarters would have been warned of its approach. It must be admitted that this division was badly posted, since it did not occupy the position which it should have occupied to fulfil its purpose of covering the country to the west of Lake Garda.

6. At Brescia was a hospital and storehouse and only three companies in garrison; they were made prisoners of war. Had the citadel been put in condition to resist open assault, this would not have hap-

pened. It was afterwards done, but should have been done before.

FRENCH GENERALS OF DIVISION.

Despinoy, Hyacinthe Francois.—Entered army as cadet 1780, second lieutenant 1784, chief of battalion 1793, general of brigade 1793, general of division 1800, died 1848. Served in the armies of the North and of the Pyrenees 1792-1795. Captured the citadel of Milan in 1796 and brevetted general of division. Governor of various fortified towns 1800-1814. In the army under the Bourbons until 1830.

"Without energy or audacity. Is not a natural soldier, is not loved by his men, does not lead them into action. Has high principles, a good mind, sound political views. A good commander in the interior."—Napoleon August 14, 1796.

Sauret, Pierre Franconin.—Born in 1742. Entered army as private in 1757, grenadier 1759, sergeant 1763, ensign 1779, captain 1792, chief of battalion, chief of brigade and general of division 1793, died 1812.

"Good, very good soldier; not sufficient intellect for a general officer; not lucky.—Napoleon August 14, 1796.

AUSTRIAN ARMY COMMANDER.

Wurmser, Count Jean Pierre de.—Born in Alsace in 1724 and entered the French army in 1745. After two years' service he moved to Vienna, entered the Austrian service, and served in the Seven Years' War. Attained the grade of division commander in 1779, and in 1787 that of corps commander. Served with distinction on the Rhine, 1793-1795. After 1797 he was made field marshal, but died the same year without further service.

ARMY OF ITALY—JULY 20, 1796.

Generals of Division	Generals of Brigade	Strength
	Joubert	
	Valette	
Massena	Rampon	15,391 incl. 2 cavalry reg.
	Victor	
	Pijon	
	Guillaume	
Augereau	Beyrand	5,368 incl. 1 cavalry reg.
	Robert	
Sauret	Guieu	4,462
	Rusca	

Serurier	Pelletier	10,000 incl. 2 cavalry reg.
	Charton	
	Serviez	
	Dallemagne	
Despinoy	Bertin	5,500
Kilmaine		1,535

Total, 42,256

The 12th *demi*-brigade was *en route* to join Serurier and the 25th *demi*-brigade was *en route* to join Despinoy from Milan; the latter was at Bergamo. These reserves would bring the strength of the army to 46,700.

SECOND CAMPAIGN

Military Situation.—The withdrawal of 25,000 men under Gen. Wurmser to reinforce the Austrian army in Italy had weakened the Austrian armies along the Rhine River and allowed the French armies to cross that river.

The French Army of the Sambre and Meuse, under Gen. Jourdan, crossed the Rhine north of the Main, and the French Army of the Rhine under Gen. Moreau at Strasburg. About the 20th of August, Jourdan was near Nuremberg and Moreau near Ulm. From Ulm, Gen. Moreau was to move a force on Innsbruck and threaten Wurmser's communications through the Inn Valley. This, it was believed by the Directory, would cause Wurmser to retreat from the Tyrol and join Archduke Charles in Germany. The Directory advised Napoleon, under these circumstances, to advance to Trent and follow Wurmser over the Brenner Pass.

Napoleon had three brigades—10,000 men—under Vaubois west of Lake Garda; two of these brigades were north of Lake Idro and one at Salo. Massena had four brigades—13,000 men—between Lake Garda and the Adige with one brigade of cavalry. Augereau had three brigades—10,000 men—at Verona. Kilmaine was at Verona with a mixed brigade of 2,000 men. Sahuguet was besieging Mantua with a force of 8,000 men. Several thousand men were sick in the hospitals.

Wurmser's regular force was now reduced to 40,000 men. A new chief of staff was sent him from Vienna to suggest a plan of operations. The plan adopted was to divide his army into two equal corps—one under Wurmser to assemble at Bassano and defend the road eastward from Verona; the other under Gen. Davidovich to remain at Trent and defend the road leading into the Tyrol. Each could advance cautiously and if Napoleon attacked either, the other could relieve Mantua and operate on the French communications.

When the campaign opened, one division of Wurmser's corps was at Bassano, one in the valley of the Brenta near Primolano, and one just east of Trent.

Davidovich was compelled to detach two brigades to protect his communications against Moreau's army and had but 14,000 regulars with some militia. His main body—8,000 men—was near Roveredo with outposts at Ala and beyond Riva; the reserve was at Trent.

Napoleon's Plan.—Napoleon notified both the Directory and Gen. Moreau that he would advance on Trent about September 2, and reach there the 4th or 5th. He would then be able to decide on his next step.

His plan was to advance in three columns. Vaubois with his two brigades was to advance to the vicinity of Riva and there meet his Salo brigade, which was to be transported by water. Massena was to advance up the Adige valley and Augereau up the valleys north of Verona.

Kilmaine was directed to hold Verona with an infantry garrison of 1,000 men and cover it with a cavalry brigade.

Sahuguet was to hold the line about Mantua and send a cavalry outpost to Legnago.

As it was possible that Napoleon himself might move north from Trent he warned both Kilmaine and Sahuguet that the Austrians might appear in force either at Legnago or Verona. If the opposing force was too great, Kilmaine and Sahuguet were to fall back behind the Oglio, leaving a strong garrison in Peschiera.

Campaign—September 2.—Vaubois advanced to Riva and Massena drove the Austrian outposts out of Ala.

September 3.—Massena captured Roveredo and drove the Austrians beyond Galliano. Vaubois united his forces and moved up the west side of the Adige.

September 4.—Napoleon entered Trent with Massena and was there joined by Vaubois.

September 5.—Massena and Vaubois attacked Davidovich at Lavis and compelled him to retreat towards Botzen. Augereau arrived at Roveredo and was sent eastwards to Levico.

September 6.—Napoleon decided to leave Vaubois at Lavis, covering Trent, while he with Massena and Augereau moved against Wurmser.

September 7.—Augereau with two brigades attacked Primolano where there was an Austrian brigade of 2,000 men and succeeded in capturing the commanding officer and most of his force.

September 8.—Massena and Augereau reached the foothills north of Bassano, where Wurmser had left a brigade on each side of the river to cover his trains near Cittadella. A third brigade was in reserve near Bassano. Massena attacked west of the river and Augereau east of the river and together carried the Austrian lines and pursued the Austrian troops to their reserves who were also defeated.

The Austrians lost 35 guns, their bridge equipage and a large number of prisoners. Some of the fugitives retreated eastwards from Cittadella, but the main force to Montebello. Napoleon had now almost completely destroyed one of Wurmser's three divisions; one after considerable loss retreated to Montebello; the third was at Montebello when Bassano was attacked and was not engaged. Wurmser himself joined this division.

September 9.—Wurmser now decided to move on Legnago, cross the river and go to Mantua. He spent the day in reorganizing and resting his troops near Arcole, but sent a cavalry force to Legnago which was at once evacuated by the French garrison. Massena followed to Montebello; Augereau moved to Padua.

September 10.—Wurmser reached Legnago in the afternoon and crossed the river. Massena's advance guard crossed at Ronco that night. Augereau marched towards Legnago.

September 11.—Sahuguet was warned of Wurmser's movements and directed to destroy all the bridges over the Molinella River between Sanguinetto and Mantua and guard the river; Kilmaine was to assist him. Massena was directed to march on Sanguinetto and Augereau was directed to take Legnago if possible. Wurmser left a strong rear guard in Legnago and started for Sanguinetto.

Napoleon's plans went astray this day. Sahuguet's men did not destroy all the bridges, and Massena's guide, instead of taking him on the direct road to Sanguinetto, took him *via* Angiari and Cerea. Massena therefore ran into Wurmser's main body with two brigades greatly weakened by stragglers and was defeated. Wurmser, guided by a native, passed over a bridge south of Sanguinetto and joined the Austrian garrison opposite Mantua. Sahuguet abandoned his investing line east of the Mincio and crossed the Mincio at Goito.

September 12.—A brigade of Massena's division and Augereau's division invested Legnago. Massena moved towards Mantua.

September 13.—The Austrian commander of Legnago surrendered with 1,600 men and the French investing troops marched on Mantua. Augereau was obliged by sickness to give up his command.

September 14 and 15.—These days were spent by Napoleon in uniting his forces and attacking Wurmser at San Giorgio to compel him to evacuate the east bank of the Mincio. The fighting was very severe but at last Napoleon was successful.

The campaign ended September 15, two weeks from the day Napoleon started from Trent. After a few days' rest, Massena was sent to occupy Verona and take post at Bassano where he could communicate with Vaubois *via* the Brenta valley. The other divisions remained near Mantua.

Wurmser took with him into Mantua about 10,000 men which added to the garrison made a force of about 25,000 men. The fighting strength of this force was reduced by several thousand on the sick report. Wurmser encamped most of his men on the main land southwest of the fortification.

Napoleon assigned Kilmaine to the command of the investing forces which he organized into two divisions under Gens. Sahuguet and Dallemagne. The investment was not at first very close but after Wurmser attempted to seize Governolo near the mouth of the Mincio, Kilmaine reinforced by Augereau's division drove him into his intrenched camp west of the Mincio. The French lines of investment were then strengthened by field fortifications.

The French army suffered greatly in this campaign. All of the brigade commanders of Massena's division were killed, wounded or so exhausted by the operations as to be on the sick report.

The distance from Rivoli to Lavis is 60 miles; from Lavis to Cittadella 70 miles, and from Cittadella to Mantua 70 miles *via* Ronco. The divisions of Massena and Augereau must therefore have marched on an average about 15 miles a day from the 2nd to the 13th inclusive, besides engaging the enemy almost daily.

On October 1, Napoleon reported to the Directory that he had 18,000 men on the sick report; 4,000 from wounds. He reported the strength of his divisions—Vaubois, 8,000; Massena, 5,500; Augereau, 5,400; Sahuguet, 4,500; Dallemagne, 4,500. The strength of the cavalry reserve is not mentioned.

1. At the beginning of September, when Wurmser moved towards Bassano, leaving Davidovich in the Tyrol, he should have directed Davidovich, in case he was attacked in force by the French, not to accept battle at Roveredo, but to retire on Bassano, in order to unite the army before giving battle. The Tyrolean militia could have guarded the Avisio valley. Otherwise he should have ordered Davidovich to retire on Galliano and the valley of the Avisio. Roveredo and the other positions occupied by him are good positions, but they cannot compensate for lack of numbers if attacked by impetuous troops. In all affairs in gorges, columns once broken, interfere with each other and fall into the power of the enemy.

2. Wurmser having united his corps at Bassano, should have sent only a column, consisting of a division of infantry, 2,000 cavalry, and a bridge train, to relieve Mantua. This force should have crossed the Adige at Albaredo from which it is only a short march to Mantua. The garrison of Mantua thus reinforced could have maintained itself in the field for some time. He himself should have retired to the Piave. The French army would have been obliged to hold its left in the Tyrol, its centre in front of the Piave, and at the same time reinforce its right in order to re-establish the blockade of Mantua. This would have been a heavy task for a small army.

3. After Bassano, Wurmser was compelled to march to the Adige with the remnant of his army. His bridge train and reserve parks having been captured, he should have been surrounded, stopped by the river and compelled to surrender. He owed his good fortune in reaching Mantua to the French chief of battalion who evacuated Legnago.

4. The Marshal made a mistake in leaving any garrison in Legnago. It was impossible for him to retreat to Legnago in the face of the entire French army; he was obliged to try to reach Mantua. It would have been easier for him to move to Milan than to return to Legnago. He reduced his own strength and sacrificed this garrison uselessly.

5. Wurmser was also wrong in risking a battle at San Giorgio; he should have retired to the country south of Mantua which is the real battlefield of the garrison of Mantua when strong enough to operate outside its walls.

He might also have crossed from this section to the country south of the Po. By making a detour, he might have reached Padua with his

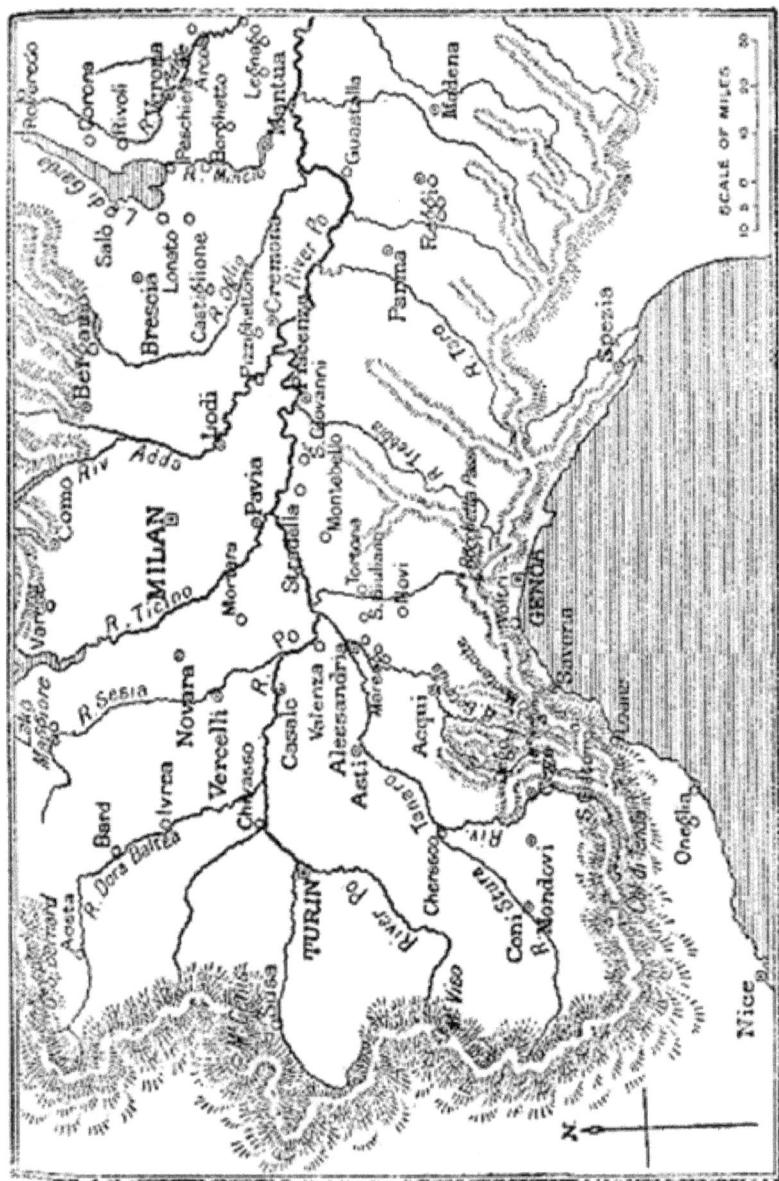

MAP TO ILLUSTRATE THE CAMPAIGNS IN NORTH ITALY

cavalry, artillery and staff before the French general became aware of his movement.

FRENCH GENERALS OF DIVISION.

Sahuguet, Jean Joseph.—Born 1756. Entered French army as lieutenant and became captain 1784; lieut. col. of dragoons 1791, general of brigade 1792, general of division 1793, died 1803. Served in the Army of the Pyrenees, in the Army of Italy and as governor of conquered provinces after Wurmser's second campaign.

Vaubois, Claude Henri.—Born 1748. Captain of artillery at the outbreak of the revolution, general of brigade 1793, general of division 1795, retired as lieutenant general 1817, died 1839. In the Army of the Alps 1793 to 1795, in the Army of Italy in 1796, in 1798 was appointed by Napoleon commander of the island of Malta which he successfully defended for two years. Elected senator and made count in 1808. Took no part in Napoleon's government in 1815 and remained in chamber of peers until his death.

"Vaubois is a brave man. Has the proper qualifications for the commander of a besieged place but not for the commander of a division in a very active army or in a war so vigorously conducted as this."—Napoleon November 24, 1796.

AUSTRIAN ARMY—JULY 26, 1796.

Wurmser—General in Chief
Weyrother—Chief of Staff.

Wing	Brigade	Bat.	Squad.	Inf.	Cav.	total
Right—	Reuss					
Quasdanovich	Spork	17	13	15,272	2,349	17,621
	Ott					
	Ocskay					
	Kummer					
Right-Centre—	Bajalics					
Melas	Nicoletti	19	4	13,676	727	14,403
	Pittoni					
Left-Centre—	Mitrokski					
Davidovich	Liptai	11	10	8,274	1,618	9,892
	Spiegel					
Left—	Hohenzollem					
Mezaros	Minkwitz	5	7	3,949	1,072	5,021
	Total			41,171	5,766	46,937

49

Napoleon and Alvinczi

Military Situation.—After the defeat of Wurmser in front of Mantua, Napoleon moved his headquarters to Milan where he remained until the middle of October.

While he was engaged in his second campaign with Wurmser, the French armies in Bavaria were defeated by Archduke Charles and both Jourdan and Moreau had retreated to the Rhine River.

Napoleon was now anxious for peace with Austria. His own army was exhausted and in no condition to invest Mantua and meet the new Austrian army which the emperor would be sure to send; his communications were harassed by Sardinian bandits who seemed to be supported by their government; both the Papal states and Naples were threatening war and an uprising in Venice was to be feared; all the other Italian states were restless and ready to desert him if he met with defeat. His requisitions had been very severe on Italy, robbing her not only of supplies and war material, but also of her most precious works of art.

On October 2, he wrote to the emperor of Austria, threatening to advance on Triest and destroy that harbour, unless peace was made. As this had no effect, on the 16th he wrote to Wurmser offering him free passage for his entire garrison if he would surrender the fortress of Mantua; this letter was not answered.

The Austrians, who had some reserve battalions on the frontier of Venice, at Tarvis and Gorz, used these and the battalions of Wurmser's army that had retired eastward, to form the nucleus of a new army. Knowing from the Venetians the weakness of Massena's division, these troops advanced to the Piave River.

On the 17th of October, Napoleon informed the Directory that the Austrians had 15,000 men on the Piave, 14,000 in the Tyrol and were sending troops from Austria to reinforce them; he urged that he be similarly reinforced.

About the middle of the month he started for Verona *via* Pavia, Modena and Bologna and reached his army October 23.

Napoleon's Plan.—Assuming that Davidovich's corps had been reduced by detachments sent to the main army on the Piave, which was daily growing in strength, Napoleon decided to have Vaubois attack Davidovich and drive him back into the mountains. Then Vaubois could either come with his whole force or send a large part of it down the Brenta valley to unite with Massena and Augereau.

Vaubois had 10,500 men at Lavis and Trent; Massena had 9,500 at Bassano and Cittadella; Augereau 8,500 at Verona, a reserve infantry brigade of 3,000 was at Villafranca and the reserve cavalry brigade of 1,600 men at Verona. Kilmaine with the divisions of Sahuguet and Dallemagne was at Mantua.

The Austrian Plan.—In the latter part of September, Gen. Alvinczi was assigned to the command of the relieving army which was strengthened as much as the resources of the empire would permit.

Having visited Davidovich in the Tyrol, he decided on the following plan. Davidovich was to recall the two brigades that had been protecting his communications in the previous campaign from possible attack by detachments from Moreau's army, and his army was to be strengthened by four brigades to 18,000 or 20,000 men. He was to assume the offensive and drive Vaubois out of Trent, thus giving the Austrians the northern end of the Brenta valley. Alvinczi was to personally command the army which was to be concentrated on the Piave River. This army was to have six brigades—28,000 to 30,000 men. He was to move from the Piave to Bassano and Cittadella and secure the southern end of the Brenta valley.

The two Austrian armies could then concentrate on either line of march, or both advance to unite at Verona.

The French and Austrian plans were similar; the Austrian forces outnumbered the French by one-half the strength of the French mobile force. To offset this advantage, the French were protected by the Adige River and its fortresses—Verona and Legnago—each of which had been placed in a good state of defence by Napoleon's chief engineer and chief of artillery.

Campaign.—November 2.—Vaubois made an unsuccessful attack on the advancing Austrian forces north of Lavis. Alvinczi's troops began to cross the Piave River.

November 3.—Davidovich advanced his left wing so as to cut Vaubois from the Brenta, and his right wing along the west side of the Adige. Alvinczi crossed the Piave River and advanced in two columns on Bassano and Cittadella.

November 4.—Davidovich, still advancing on both sides of the Adige, compelled Vaubois to retreat to Galliano. Alvinczi advanced on Bassano and Cittadella and Massena retreated to Vicenza where the reserve infantry brigade joined him. Augereau advanced from Verona to Montebello.

While authorizing Massena to retreat, Napoleon had not given up his plan of holding the line of the Brenta. He therefore reinforced Massena and pushed Augereau to the front.

November 5.—Davidovich took possession of Trent and arranged his columns for an advance on Calliano.

Alvinczi crossed the Brenta unopposed. Massena was at Vicenza; Augereau advanced to that point.

Gen. Joubert, whose brigade was at Legnago, was ordered to Rivoli with one *demi*-brigade to cover the retreat of Vaubois.

November 6.—Vaubois was attacked on the afternoon of the 6th at Calliano and resisted the attack. The Austrian brigade west of the Adige, having only a small force in its front, reached the Riva-Rovere-do road and threatened his communications.

Massena and Augereau, under Napoleon's supervision, attacked Alvinczi between Cittadella and Bassano on the Brenta. Both armies fought well. Napoleon was unable to force Alvinczi to recross the Brenta.

November 7.—Vaubois fought all day at Galliano. Being obliged to send troops to protect his communications, he was decisively defeated in the afternoon and retreated that night through Ala to Peri. Joubert's brigade moved up from Rivoli and held Corona.

Napoleon had intended to renew the battle on the Brenta this day, but the news from Vaubois made him hesitate and he finally started Massena for Verona to be followed by Augereau. In person he hastened to Rivoli and put Vaubois' troops in position at that place.

November 8.—Massena reached Verona in person on the afternoon of the 8th and as he was familiar with the country was placed temporarily in command of Vaubois' division, with orders to defend the line between Lake Garda and the Adige. Massena sent another *de-*

mi-brigade to Joubert at Corona and posted the remainder of Vaubois' division at Rivoli. Davidovich did not push his pursuit.

Massena's division retired to Verona and Augereau's to Montebello. Alvinczi reached Vicenza.

November 9.—Davidovich, having been informed that Massena had reinforced Vaubois, ceased his advance. Vaubois and Massena strengthened their positions at Corona and Rivoli with artillery and intrenchments.

Augereau's division returned to Verona where he was assigned the defence of the Adige from Verona to Legnago. Alvinczi advanced to Montebello.

November 10.—The Austrians did not move this day and the French simply strengthened their lines.

November 11.—Alvinczi advanced to Villanova from which place the French outpost retired. An Austrian reconnoitring force came within a mile of Verona but was driven back.

As everything was quiet in Vaubois' front, Napoleon decided to again attack Alvinczi. Massena in person was recalled from Rivoli and that night the division of Massena and part of that of Augereau moved out and encamped near the east gate of Verona.

November 12.—At break of day Napoleon moved from Verona and attacked the Austrian advance brigades at Caldiero—8,000 men— with the divisions of Massena and a part of that of Augereau. Although the resistance was obstinate, the Austrians being in intrenched villages. Napoleon was making progress when, in the afternoon, two additional Austrian brigades reached the field. The French were then defeated and driven with considerable loss back into Verona. The darkness probably prevented the Austrians from following up their success.

November 13.—There were no operations this day, though Davidovich was preparing to advance.

Napoleon was thoroughly discouraged and wrote a very despondent letter to the Directory. Vaubois' division had lost a third of its strength and some of its regiments had shown signs of demoralization. Massena and Augereau had twice unsuccessfully attacked the enemy and had suffered severe loss. The Austrians were now relatively much stronger than they had been at the opening of the campaign. Retreat to the Adda seemed the only thing left.

November 14.—Another day passed without any operations. Davidovich made preparations to attack Corona on the 15th. Alvinczi decided to throw a bridge across the Adige south of Caldiero and was making causeways through the marsh to the site of the bridge.

Napoleon's spirits rose and he began to despise an adversary who was so slow to take advantage of his opportunities. He knew that Vaubois could not hold out against Davidovich and yet he did not dare to move Massena and Augereau to Rivoli with Alvinczi at the gates of Verona. He therefore decided to strike the communications of Alvinczi about a day's march from Verona, and see if he could not make him retreat and give Napoleon time to destroy Davidovich.

At Villanova, thirteen miles east of Verona, the Verona-Vicenza highway is hemmed in between the foothills of the Alps on the north and the marshy triangle between the Adige and Alpon. Alvinczi left his trains just east of Villanova.

Napoleon knew that Alvinczi would feel sensitive about this point, and he therefore made up his mind to threaten it.

To secure a striking force, he directed Gen. Vaubois to send at once two of his seven *demi*-brigades from Rivoli to Ronco and one to Verona, and on the 15th to concentrate his entire division at Rivoli, leaving only an outpost at Corona. Kilmaine was informed that he must keep Wurmser in Mantua, Alvinczi out of Verona, and send one of his seven *demi*-brigades to Napoleon.

Sixteen miles below Verona on the west bank of the Adige River is the small village of Ronco, where the French had a *ponton* bridge which had been dismantled a few days before. Between the Adige and Alpon is marsh, below the water level of the two rivers. A dike along the east bank of the Adige and another along the west bank of the Alpon were the principal roadways in this section. There was a small area of high ground near the junction of the two rivers. At Arcole or Areola, where the Alpon is about 60 feet wide, there was a narrow wooden bridge. Arcole is only three and a half miles from Villanova and due south of it.

After dark on the 16th, Napoleon, with the divisions of Massena and Augereau, Gen. Guieu's brigade of Vaubois' division and a brigade of cavalry, marched down to Ronco where orders had been given to rebuild the bridge. *En route*, one of Guieu's *demi*-brigades was left opposite Alvinczi's proposed crossing. An Austrian battalion, posted at Ronco, retreated to Arcole.

November 15.—As directed, Vaubois withdrew from Corona without being attacked and concentrated his remaining troops at Rivoli. Davidovich followed with four brigades and occupied Corona.

At daylight, Massena crossed the bridge, and with part of his division, started up the pike for Caldiero. The Austrians at once sent a force to meet him but in the course of the day Massena reached and held Porcil a small village a mile and a half from the Verona-Vicenza road.

Augereau followed Massena and moved on the dike to Arcole, where there was an Austrian brigade with two guns. For a mile, this dike was separated from the Austrians behind the opposite dike by the width of the river—30 yards. The flank fire of the Austrians threw Augereau's column in disorder and, although at one time he was in actual possession of the bridge, he could not hold it.

In the afternoon, Napoleon sent Guieu with his brigade to Albaredo to cross in boats to come up on the Austrians' left flank. The attacks on the bridge were continued by Augereau's column until late in the afternoon. As at Lodi, the generals of division and brigade, placed themselves at the head of the column to carry it forward, but all in vain; Napoleon himself led one attack. Towards evening Napoleon ordered both divisions to recross the *ponton* bridge leaving a strong guard on the east bank.

Guieu came up after dark and captured Arcole by surprise. He stayed there until midnight. Hearing nothing from Napoleon, he then retreated to Albaredo, crossed the river and returned to Ronco.

While the day's work had not been entirely successful, it did cause Alvinczi to send his trains from Villanova to Montebello; to give up all thought of crossing the Adige; and led him to engage in a battle on the dikes.

That night Napoleon ordered Vaubois to still further reduce his force and send 1,000 men into Verona to replace some he had ordered to Ronco.

November 16.—Davidovich spent this day in making preparations to attack Rivoli. Alvinczi sent two brigades down the dikes from Porcil and four brigades to Arcole. One of the latter took possession of Albaredo and protected that flank; one remained in Arcole; the other two crossed the Alpon and marched towards the French *ponton* bridge. Alvinczi hoped to prevent the French from again crossing the river.

Massena and Augereau crossed the river as on the preceding day, and met the Austrians on both dikes close to the bridge. The battle of the dikes was maintained all day long without the capture of the bridge at Arcole. In the afternoon, the French made an attempt to bridge the Alpon near its mouth but the Austrians on the opposite dike prevented its successful completion.

At night Napoleon again withdrew Massena and Augereau to the west bank, leaving a strong guard to cover the bridge.

November 17.—Davidovich attacked Vaubois, routed him and captured two of his three brigade commanders and a third of his command. Vaubois fled with the remnant of his command to Castelnovo. Davidovich stopped between Rivoli and Castelnovo to await orders from Alvinczi.

On the night of the 16th-17th, Napoleon sent a battalion of infantry and a regiment of cavalry to Legnago, to form with its garrison a column which was to move up the east side of the Adige to Arcole. Preparations were also made for the construction of a bridge near the mouth of the Alpon on the following day.

In crossing the river on the morning of November 17, Massena was in advance and was for a time cut off with a part of his division, by the breaking of the *ponton* bridge. The French artillery however protected him from the attacks of the Austrians who were again marching for the bridge.

Severe fighting on the dikes again took place beginning near the bridge and with varying success. In the afternoon Augereau, however, crossed the Alpon near its mouth and formed a junction with the Legnago column. Massena then attacked along both dikes. Augereau was repulsed in an attack on Arcole and the day might have ended with the village in the possession of the Austrians, had not Napoleon sent a small squad of cavalry, in concealment around the Austrian left flank, where its bugles sounded calls, which made the Austrian commander believe a large cavalry force was on his flank. He therefore abandoned Arcole and retired through Gazzolo. Augereau and Massena pursued and attacked but were repulsed.

The French bivouacked on both sides the Alpon at Arcole.

November 18.—Davidovich did not move, as he had heard nothing from Alvinczi. Massena and Augereau moved up on opposite sides of the Alpon to Villanova, and caused the withdrawal of the last of Alvinczi's forces. They then marched to Verona, while the cavalry followed Alvinczi towards Montebello.

Napoleon, having heard that Vaubois' force was almost destroyed, ordered Massena to unite with the remnants of Vaubois' division at Villafranca.

November 19.—On the afternoon of this day, Davidovich learned of Alvinczi's retreat, and began himself to move northwards. Massena moved to Villafranca while Augereau remained at Verona.

November 20.—Massena organized his force at Villafranca. Alvinczi this day learned of the defeat of Vaubois and informed Davidovich that the main army would again move on Verona.

November 21.—Massena moved on Rivoli, and Augereau up the east bank of the Adige. Hearing that Massena was moving to attack him, and Augereau was marching for his communications, Davidovich hastened to retreat. Massena struck his rear guard at Rivoli and Augereau's advance guard struck him in flank at Peri.

November 22.—Davidovich sent word to Alvinczi that his troops were in no condition to continue the campaign, and he would retire to Roveredo. Alvinczi had by this time retaken his position at Caldiero and Arcole.

November 23.—Alvinczi received Davidovich's message and not caring to face Napoleon alone, promptly ordered a retreat to the Brenta River. Napoleon made no attempt to pursue, as his troops needed rest. Assuming that the relieving armies were nearby, Wurmser made a sortie this day but was repulsed.

This ended the three weeks' campaign.

NAPOLEON'S COMMENTS.

1. When Alvinczi began his campaign he decided to move in two columns. Nothing could have been more faulty than this plan. As soon as he was master of Bassano, he should have ordered Davidovich to join him and appear on the Adige with a united army. The defence of the Tyrol might have been left to the militia.

2. In occupying Caldiero, he should have established strong posts in the marshes opposite Ronco. In assuming that the marshes were impassable he allowed the French to construct a bridge at Ronco and place an army in his rear.

3. The columns of Alvinczi and Davidovich, although only ten or twelve leagues apart, were unable to communicate with each other. The country above Verona is very rough and has no practicable cross roads.

4. It is said that my bridge should have been made at Albaredo instead of Ronco. This is wrong. In Verona, Kilmaine had a force of only 1,500 men; the town might have been taken by assault. After crossing the river Massena was at once sent up the Adige, to place himself in

rear of Alvinczi. If the Austrian commander now advanced on Verona, Massena could pursue him. If the bridge had been constructed at Albaredo, this river and the marshes would have protected Alvinczi while attacking Verona. The passage at Ronco was audacious but not dangerous, while that at Albaredo would have been both rash and dangerous. It would have compromised the safety of Verona.

5. Why did Napoleon retreat behind the Adige on the nights of the first and second days? To remove the bridge and intercept Davidovich on the road to Mantua if necessary. If Davidovich reached Mantua first, all would have been lost, but if the French army reached there first, all would have been safe. United with Vaubois, the general in chief would have defeated Davidovich, driven him back to the Tyrol, and been back on the Adige before Alvinczi could have crossed.

6. It is said a bridge should have been thrown over the Alpon on the first, certainly on the second day. No, it was only on the third day that the Austrian army was sufficiently discouraged to warrant it. Even then the generals thought the movement of the army into the plain east of the Alpon was too hazardous. It must be remembered that the French army had been weakened by the battles of the Brenta and Caldiero and by the first and second days of Arcole.

AUSTRIAN ARMY COMMANDER.

Alvinczi, Baron Joseph.—Born in Transylvania, 1735. Distinguished himself in the Seven Years' War and attained the rank of brigade commander. In 1789 he commanded a division in the war with the Turks. From 1792 to 1796 he served with distinction in the Netherlands and on the Rhine. In 1808 was made field marshal and died in 1810.

ARMY OF ITALY.—NOV. 12, 1796.

Generals of Division	Generals of Brigade	Strength
	Menard	
	Rampon	
Massena	Vial	9,540 inc. 2 regt. of cavalry
	Pijon	
	Leclerc	
	Verdier	
Augereau	Bon	8,340 inc. 1 regt. of cavalry
	Lannes	
	Guieu	
Vaubois	Fiorella	10,500

	Gardanne	
	Chabot	
	Dallemagne	
Kilmaine	Sandos	8,830 inc. 1 regt. of cavalry
Sahuguet	Lebley	
	Bertin	
Macquart	(infantry reserve)	2,750 inc. 1 regt of cavalry
Dumas	(cavalry reserve)	1,600—6 regt. of cavalry
	Total	41,560

SECOND CAMPAIGN.

Military Situation—Immediately after the retreat of Alvinczi, Napoleon made Joubert brevet general of division and assigned him to the command of Vaubois' divison, whose numerical strength was restored by reinforcements, with orders to hold the positions of Corona and Rivoli. Intrenchments and batteries were constructed at Corona, at Rivoli to command the road connecting plateau and river, and on the east bank of the Adige at the gorge of the river below Rivoli. Massena was posted at Verona with orders to support Joubert, and Augereau was charged with the defence of the Adige from Ronco southwards.

The nucleus of a new division was begun at Desenzano, by placing a brigade of infantry and some cavalry under the command of Gen. Rey, who had reported from the Army of the Vendé, with reinforcements. He was to protect the country west of Lake Garda. He had a detachment at Lake Idro, some battalions at Salo, and a detachment at Brescia.

Kilmaine, having become incapacitated for field service, was assigned to the general command of the region between the Chiese and Ticino, and Serurier was recalled from Tuscany to take command of the besieging forces around Mantua. Kilmaine still retained the general command of the cavalry of the army. Vaubois was again sent to command the French troops in Tuscany.

Sahuguet being detached to command one of the fortresses in the rear, Gen. Dumas of the cavalry was temporarily assigned to command his division.

Napoleon employed the period between his first and second campaigns against Alvinczi in perfecting his organization.

In each of his principal divisions, the old and the inefficient officers were ordered to their homes and replaced by the young officers who had shown the greatest bravery and activity.

The field and horse artillery were reorganized and equipped.

Field works were constructed at exposed points and the permanent works were strengthened by more artillery.

A system of signals, by cannon located at intervals, was arranged so that warning could be rapidly sent from one division to another announcing the appearance of the enemy and whether or not assistance was desired. Courier posts were established for the rapid transmission of orders in all directions.

Napoleon spent most of his time between the campaigns at Milan, but was *en route* to Bologna when the campaign opened.

Austrian Plan.—After his first campaign. Gen. Alvinczi concentrated the greater part of his army at Roveredo, leaving a force of 5,000 at Bassano under Gen. Bajalich and a force of 10,000 at Padua under Gen. Provera. His own force numbered about 28,000, excluding the required garrisons and small detachments guarding his communications.

He was urged to relieve Wurmser at once, notwithstanding the inclement weather, as the garrison of Mantua was reported to be almost out of rations and would soon be compelled to surrender.

His plan was to divide his Roveredo force into six brigades. One was to follow the shore of Lake Garda and join the others in front of Rivoli; two were to follow the mountain road through Corona; two were to follow the west bank of the Adige; and one the east bank. The latter was to throw a bridge across the river below Rivoli. The field artillery and the cavalry were to follow the river roads.

To disconcert the French, Provera was to move first and threaten Legnago. He was provided with a bridge train so that he could cross the Adige out of range of that place and relieve Mantua, whose garrison was, if necessary, to retreat across the Po and join the Papal forces.

Bajalich was to move second and threaten Verona and prevent its garrison from moving to either flank.

French Forces.—Joubert's division of 10,300 men had its reserves at Rivoli and its outposts guarding all the lines of approach to Rivoli; one brigade was at Corona. Massena, with 9,000 men, was at Verona; Augereau with 9,000 was guarding the Adige with his troops widely scattered from Verona to Legnago; Rey with 4,000 men was at Desenzano and Salo. In addition to these forces there was a cavalry brigade in front of Augereau at Legnago, one in rear of Verona, and a third at Villafranca. A *demi*-brigade of infantry, 2,000 men, under Gen. Victor, was also at Villafranca. The investing force at Mantua was about 10,000 men.

The Campaign.—*January 7.*—Gen. Provera started from Padua and marched to Este.

Napoleon was in Milan.

January 8.—Provera marched towards Legnago and Bajalich left Bassano. Augereau was informed of Provera's movement and prepared to defend the Adige. Napoleon was on his way to Bologna.

January 9.—Provera attacked Augereau's advance posts about five miles east of Legnago and drove them back to the Adige. Bajalich was marching towards Verona. Napoleon probably reached Bologna on the night of the 9th.

January 10.—Provera waited for his brigade and wagon trains. Bajalich appeared in front of Verona and at Arcole, and sent some troops into the mountains north of Verona to get in touch with the main column. His outposts in front of Verona were attacked by Massena's cavalry and retired to Caldiero. Alvinczi started the three brigades which were to move along the lake and on the plateau, for Rivoli.

Napoleon was at Bologna, where he had assembled a brigade under Gen. Lannes to hold the town against the Papal troops who were advancing northward. Having heard from Augereau that the Austrians were in force in front of Legnago, he at once sent these troops, *via* Ferrara, to defend the Adige below Legnago.

January 11.—Provera ordered a reconnaissance of the river at Angiari where he decided to cross the Adige. Bajalich made no movement. Alvinczi's second and third brigades moved towards Corona while his first continued its march down the lake. His fourth brigade reached the Adige opposite Corona.

Napoleon was still at Bologna where he met the representatives of the Duke of Tuscany.

January 12.—Provera ordered a bridge to be thrown over the Adige at Angiari, but afterwards revoked the order. Bajalich attacked Massena's outpost close to Verona and captured it. He was in turn attacked by Massena and forced back to Caldiero. Alvinczi's second and third brigades reached Corona in the morning, but through a misunderstanding only one attacked. The small brigade of French troops, under the personal supervision of Joubert, stationed there, being well

61

intrenched, was able to hold its own. The fourth of Alvinczi's brigades was now ordered to ascend the plateau and join the second and third.

Napoleon left Bologna on the night of the 11th and reached Roverbella on the morning of the 12th. From the reports received, he assumed that Provera's was the main attack. He therefore decided to concentrate on him, cross the Adige, and attack him.

Massena was ordered to hold himself in readiness to move on Legnago; Victor's reserve infantry *demi*-brigade and the reserve cavalry brigade were ordered to the road between Legnago and Mantua; Rey was directed to leave a sufficient force at Salo to meet any force coming down the west side of Lake Garda and march to Valeggio with a *demi*-brigade.

Napoleon then went to Verona, where he arrived in time to witness Massena's counter attack.

January 13.—On the 13th, Provera concentrated his force near Legnago as if to attack and sent a party some miles down the river as if to secure a crossing. After dark he moved to Angiari above Legnago, sent a force across in boats to drive out the small garrison, and began the construction of a *ponton* bridge.

Bajalich remained at Caldiero and in the morning defeated a cavalry force sent on a reconnaissance by Napoleon. At Provera's request, in the afternoon he went to Arcole to threaten a crossing. Alvinczi's second, third and fourth brigades advanced through Corona and deployed along the Tasso occupying the villages of Caprino and Martino. The first brigade had only reached Lumini. The Austrian columns following the Adige valley were on the same general line as those on the plateau.

During the night of January 12-13, Joubert was informed by his outposts near Lumini that an Austrian force was advancing to that point. Leaving his fires burning he retired from Corona in the early morning and withdrew his forces to the southern ridge north-west of Rivoli; only observation posts were left on the northern ridge. In retiring from Corona, a detached battalion was overlooked and was later captured by the Austrians.

Towards evening, Joubert decided that he was too weak to hold his position and gave orders to retire to Castelnovo after dark.

Before his troops had moved, however, he received word from Napoleon that he was coming in person to Rivoli and was sending Joubert reinforcements to enable him to hold his position.

Napoleon was at Verona that day and was uncertain from which point to expect the main attack. He knew that Joubert had been compelled to evacuate Corona and that a large force had appeared in front of Legnago. He had determined to send Massena and Rey to reinforce one of his flanks, but it was not until 3 p. m. that the reports clearly indicated that the main attack was from the north.

Napoleon was thoroughly familiar with the topography of the country and knew that at this season of the year the columns marching down on Rivoli, *via* the plateau, could be infantry only with a few mountain guns, that the field guns and cavalry could only reach Rivoli by the river roads. If he could, with Joubert's division, prevent the Austrians from securing the road between the river and the plateau until reinforcements could reach him, he felt that he could defeat Alvinczi's plan, since neither Bajalich nor Provera seemed strong enough to cross the Adige.

At 3 p. m. he sent orders to Gen. Victor to move from the Legnago-Mantua road *via* Villafranca to Rivoli. Victor fortunately however started on a more direct and shorter road.

At 5 p. m. he ordered Massena to leave 3,000 of his division at Verona and send three *demi*-brigades—6,000 men—as soon as possible to reinforce Joubert. Orders were at the same time sent to Rey to march with a *demi*-brigade from Valeggio to Castelnovo, where he would meet a staff officer to guide him, and if the Salo garrison was not threatened, he was to send a part of it to cross Lake Garda in boats.

Massena was probably 17 miles from the field; Rey and Victor were still further; time was necessary for the transmission of the orders and the preparation of the troops for the march. None could reach Rivoli until the following day.

That night Napoleon himself went to Rivoli and reached Joubert at 2 a. m.

January 14.—Provera crossed the river and started for Mantua. Augereau's troops, guarding the river between Verona and Angiari under Gen. Guieu, moved down and by their attacks delayed his movements. Augereau himself was at Legnago; he directed Lannes to move up to that place.

On the morning of January 14, Alvinczi had three brigades in front of Joubert and one at Lumini. His fifth brigade was on the river road with the cavalry and artillery, ready to ascend the plateau as soon as its path was cleared. The sixth brigade was still across the Adige, but could easily join the others by throwing a bridge across the river.

Alvinczi was not satisfied with the advantage he had gained and instead of ordering his first brigade from Lumini to Caprino, ordered it to march *via* Costermano and Affi to seize the ridge south of Rivoli. This would delay his attack until the afternoon. In the morning the three brigades in front of Joubert were to complete their deployment and occupy the ridge from Ceredele to San Marco.

When Napoleon reached Rivoli, it was moonlight and he was able to reconnoitre the position. He at once decided that to prevent the union of the Austrian columns, Joubert must hold the ridge at San Marco and extend his left along the ridge towards Trombalora. Even if driven from this advanced position he would gain time for the arrival of Massena and Victor.

At dawn, Joubert left 1,500 men to hold his second line and man the fortifications commanding the river road, and with about 8,500 moved out to the line selected by Napoleon. He conducted the right of his line in person. He had hardly reached San Marco before an Austrian brigade approached to occupy it. This brigade was attacked and after a severe engagement was driven back.

On the Trombalora ridge the French line was outflanked by the right brigade of the Austrian line and Joubert's left wing was defeated and retreated in a panic. The Austrians were rolling up the centre when Massena appeared with his first *demi*-brigade. Massena at once attacked the Austrian brigade in flank, drove it from the field and re-established the French left.

Before the arrival of Massena, Alvinczi saw the French left retreating and sent his centre and left brigades against Joubert at San Marco. This attack compelled Joubert to fall back to the southern ridge while Massena was restoring the left of his line on the northern ridge.

Arriving at the head of the road leading down into the Adige valley with Joubert, Napoleon saw that his fortified line in the valley was carried and the Austrians were advancing up the road in a dense column, whose head had reached the plateau.

A regiment of cavalry held in reserve charged the head of the Austrian column and was supported by Joubert with such infantry as he could rally. This attack, supported by artillery, was successful and the Austrians retreated to the valley to reform.

Then, turning to the Austrian brigades which had followed him from San Marco, Joubert held them in front while Massena, who had been joined by his second *demi*-brigade, attacked them in flank. The

64

Austrians were in turn surprised and a sudden charge of French cavalry caused them to break and retire to their morning position.

The first Austrian brigade had pursued its way unmolested and was now on the ridge south of Rivoli.

Leaving Joubert to face the Austrians north of him, Massena took one *demi*-brigade to attack this brigade. In marching to the attack, he was joined by his third *demi*-brigade, which he had sent *via* Garda to reconnoitre the road along the lake leading to Peschiera. Finding no Austrians at Garda, this brigade marched to Rivoli.

The commander of the Austrian brigade tried to retreat *via* Affi, running the gauntlet between Massena and Victor, who was approaching Affi from the south. Many of his command were captured and those who escaped ran into and were captured by Gen. Murat who had crossed the lake from Salo with its garrison and had landed at Torri.

The Austrian brigades which had recrossed the Tasso north of Rivoli were not pursued since night was falling and Napoleon had just learned that Provera had crossed the Adige at Angiari.

Napoleon now considered Alvinczi defeated and at once ordered two *demi*-brigades of Massena's division and Victor's *demi*-brigade to make a night march to Mantua to assist Serurier.

Of Massena's division, one *demi*-brigade, and of Rey's division, Murat's battalions of the Salo garrison, remained with Joubert. A *demi*-brigade of Rey's division was *en route* for the field from Valeggio and would be up the in morning.

January 15.—On the 15th, Provera continued his march for Mantua, but was delayed *en route* by the reserve cavalry brigade and Gen. Guieu.

He sent his advance guard to communicate with Wurmser, but the commander of this guard found the French investing force strongly intrenched and being himself repulsed was unable to communicate with Wurmser.

Augereau, reinforced by Lannes, moved up to Angiari to attack the rear guard left by Provera to protect his bridge. This rear guard attempted to join the main body, but was cut off and captured. Augereau then burned the Austrian bridge and started for Mantua.

That night Napoleon was at Roverbella with two *demi*-brigades of the command which had marched from Rivoli; the other *demi*-brigade was *en route* from Castelnovo.

Joubert, on the morning of the 15th, had in his front only three

Austrian brigades. He had been reinforced as above stated from the divisions of Massena and Rey, and was directed by Napoleon to take the offensive.

He first took the hill at San Marco shortly after daylight; then, pivoting on that hill, tiuned the Austrian right. He thus cut their line of retreat to Corona and compelled the Austrians to retreat over the mountains to the Adige. His victory was decisive and he captured several thousand prisoners. This closed the two days' Battle of Rivoli.

January 16.—Provera appeared before Mantua in the morning, and was here attacked by Massena, Victor, Guieu and Serurier. Being cut off from Mantua with no hope of retreat, he surrendered his remaining force of 7,000 men at 11 a. m. This engagement was known as the Battle of Favorita.

This ended the eight days' campaign. Alvinczi retreated to Roveredo and Bajalich to Bassano.

Alvinczi had sent a small raiding force down the west side of Lake Garda; this reached the vicinity of Brescia but was then compelled to retreat without doing any damage.

On February 2, Wurmser surrendered Mantua. General Wurmser with his staff, the general officers with their staffs, and an escort of 700 men were allowed to return to Austria. The remaining 15,000 became prisoners of war. A large part of the Austrian garrison died of fever during the siege.

NAPOLEON'S COMMENTS.

1. Alvinczi had for the campaign of Rivoli about 50,000 men and 120 pieces of artillery. He moved one half of his army, with all his artillery, down the valley of the Adige. The column on the east bank was stopped by a hundred men in the fort controlling the gorge of the Adige below Rivoli. The column which followed the west bank of the Adige was on the narrow shelf between the bluffs and the river. Its only exit was the road which ascends the bluffs at the plateau of Rivoli near the chapel of San Marco. This road is commanded on the north side by the height of San Marco and on the south by the plateau of Rivoli. With 25,000 men, without artillery and cavalry, Alvinczi expected to drive back the French army from Corona to Rivoli and there unite with the columns which moved along the valley. He believed that he would have only the division of Joubert to overcome and therefore again separated his command, sending one column down between Lake Garda and the mountains. Such a plan would be correct if ar-

mies were like mountains, immovable. This was the mistake frequently made by the Austrians. In this case it was assumed that Massena would remain quietly at Verona. It assumed that Napoleon did not appreciate the value of the position at Rivoli.

2. What should Alvinczi have done? Marched his army so as to permit him to fight it every day, every hour. His whole force should have marched between Lake Garda and the Adige, united by communications and acting as a single mass. Similarly he should have united his cavalry, since cavalry can go wherever infantry can. He should have made his dispositions to attack Joubert only on the morning of the attack, when he had full information as to his troops and dispositions.

3. It is a principle of war to make no detachments on the eve of making an attack, since the condition of things may change by the retreat of the enemy, or the arrival of reinforcements which will enable him to take up the offensive and render dangerous the premature dispositions that have been made.

4. One is often deceived in war as to the strength of the enemy; prisoners know only their corps, officers make uncertain reports.

5. This axiom will remedy everything. Let an army be every day, every night, every hour ready to oppose all the resistance it is capable of offering. To this end soldiers must always have their arms and ammunition; infantry should always have its artillery, cavalry , and its generals; the different divisions should be constantly disposed to support each other; in camps, at halts, on the march, the troops should always be in favourable positions, which have the qualities demanded by a field of battle, *viz.*, flanks supported and all the arms in the position best suited for them. For this purpose, there must be advance guards and flankers, far enough off to allow the main corps to deploy.

6. A great captain should ask himself several times each day, what would I do if the enemy suddenly appeared on my front, on my right flank, on my left flank? If he finds himself embarrassed to answer these questions, as a rule he is badly placed and should correct his position. If Alvinczi had said, "What if I meet the French army before I reach Rivoli, when I have but half my infantry without cavalry or artillery?" he would have replied, "I shall be beaten by forces inferior to my own." Why was not he made more careful by Lodi, Castiglione, the Brenta and Arcole?

7. Alvinczi debouched in January. Mantua was held at bay. He operates with two columns; the first from the north commanded by

himself; the other on the lower Adige, commanded by Provera. The success of Provera would be of no value, were Alvinczi defeated. This fault was aggravated by a central attack on Verona, which had no other end than that of weakening the main attacks. It is true the Austrian authorities ordered Wurmser, in case he was relieved by Provera, to cross the Po and retreat on Rome. Unless, however, he could count on the assistance of the king of Naples, this movement would have been of no value.

8. Having succeeded in throwing a bridge over the Adige, Provera should have ordered the force threatening Verona to join him; this would have greatly strengthened him. As it was, he not only left this force behind, but he also left a guard at his bridge which he should have taken up. The guard was captured. On arriving before Mantua in the morning, he should at once have forced an entrance. He did nothing that day; in the evening Napoleon with the troops from Rivoli began to arrive and on the following day he was obliged to capitulate. The Austrians did not appreciate the value of time.

9. Napoleon should have occupied the plateaus of Rivoli, Corona, San Marco and Rocca d'Anfo, by good fortifications in wood and masonry. In six weeks these four forts might have been constructed. Each with a garrison of 400 or 500 men and 15 guns would have protected these places from surprise. They would have been worth more to the army than a reinforcement of 15,000 men.

French Generals of Division.

Joubert, Barthelemy Catherine.—Born 1769. Entered volunteers as sergeant 1791; general of brigade 1795; general of division 1797; 1798 commanded in succession the armies of Holland, Mayence and Italy. Resigned this last command but was reappointed in 1799 after the army had suffered many reverses and was killed in his battle at Novi, August 1799. Served in Army of Italy 1795-97.

"He was bold, vigilant, active. Had he lived he would have attained great military renown."—Napoleon at St. Helena.

Rey, Antoine Gabriel.—Born 1768. Enlisted in army under Louis XVI, lieutenant 1791, general of brigade 1793, general of division 1795. Served with distinction in armies of the Rhine, of the West and of Italy. He did not approve of the *coup d'etat* by means of which Napoleon made himself First Consul and was relieved from command. Restored in 1808 and served in Spain from 1808 to 1814. In 1815 was commander of Valenciennes which he defended after Waterloo.

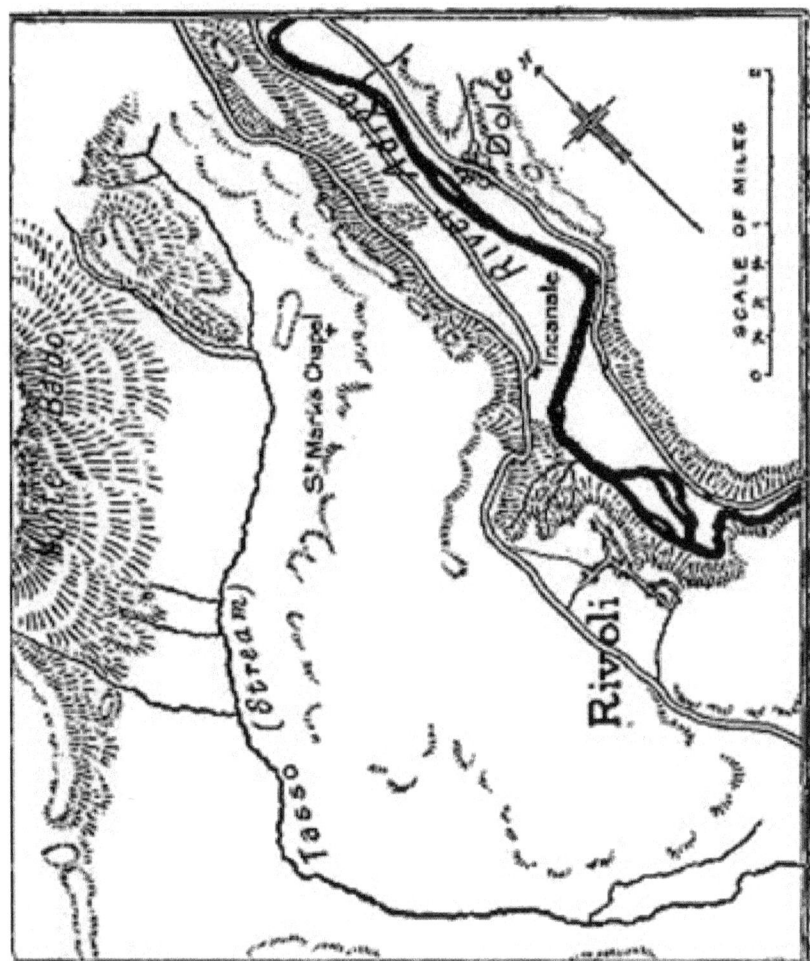

NEIGHBOURHOOD OF RIVOLI

Retired from service 1820. Died 1836.

Alvinczi—General in Chief.

Corps	Brigades	Strength
Provera	Hohenzollem, Roselmini, Liptai Schubirz, Brabeck, Pittoni	28,699
Davidovich	Laudon, Ocskay, Spork, Vukassevich	18,427

Total, 47,125

ARMY OF ITALY—JANUARY 1, 1797.

Generals of Division	Generals of Brigade	Strength
	Monnier	
Massena	Brune	8,851 inc. 2 regt. of cavalry
	Leclerc	
	Guieu	
Augereau	Point	8,851 inc. 4 regt. of cavalry
	Verdier	
	Walther	
	Vial	
Joubert (bvt.)	Lebley	10,250 inc. 1 regt of cavalry
	Sandos	
	Murat	
Rey	Vaux	4,156 inc. 2 regt. of cavalry
	Baraguey-d'Hilliers	
	Davin	
Serurier	Miollis	
Dumas	Monteau	10,230 inc. 2 regt. of cavalry
Dallemagne	Serviez	
	Lasalcette	
Cavalry reserve	Dugua	658 2 regiments
Infantry reserve	Victor	1,800 inc. 1 regt. of cavalry
	Lannes	4,000

Total, 48,610

Napoleon and Archduke Charles

Military Situation.—The second campaign against Alvinczi terminated on the 17th of January and on the following day detachments
were made from the divisions of Massena, Augereau and the cavalry
to unite with Victor's brigade near Ferrera and form a division for the
invasion of the Papal states. This division was to be commanded by
Gen. Victor.

Napoleon's next step was to clear the Brenta valley of Austrians.
On January 20, Massena's division moved to Vicenza and Augereau's
to Padua. From these positions they moved to Bassano and Cittadella.
Massena pushed detachments up the Brenta valley. This movement
caused Alvinczi with a large part of his command to retreat from
Roveredo to the Piave *via* Feltre and enabled Joubert to reoccupy
Trent and Lavis without opposition

When Wurmser surrendered Mantua on February 2, Joubert was
at Trent, Massena at Bassano, Augereau at Castelfranca and Napoleon
with Victor at Bologna.

After the surrender, Augereau was sent in person to present the
sixty colours, captured in Mantua, to the French government and
Rey was directed to escort the prisoners to the French frontier. Gen.
Guieu succeeded to the command of Augereau's division and Gen.
Baraguey-d'Hilliers to the troops of Rey's division that remained with
the army.

Napoleon continued his movement against the Papal states. Without opposition Victor moved down to Ancona on the Adriatic Sea
and thence over the mountains towards Rome. *En route* to Rome,
Napoleon was met by the Papal representatives and on February 19,
came to terms with them. He at once made arrangements to hold the
Papal states east of the Apennines, now under French protection, by
small garrisons and withdraw his main body as soon as the conditions

of the treaty were fulfilled. He personally returned to the army to begin a new campaign.

As a result of Napoleon's persistent applications for reinforcements, and because of his uninterrupted victories, the Directory in November ordered twelve *demi*-brigades—thirty-six battalions under Gens. Bernadotte and Delmas—to be sent him from the armies in France. The last of these troops were now reaching the Quadrilateral and Napoleon was anxious to begin his new campaign before the Austrian army could be similarly reinforced. When the reinforcements reached him the battalions were about 600 men each.

Napoleon's general plan was to divide his army into two wings. Joubert with about 20,000 men was to be left at Trent to await orders. Napoleon with about 40,000 was to advance in the plain between the mountains and the Adriatic on the roads leading to Triest.

The campaign opened on the 10th of March when the French troops were posted as follows: The divisions of Joubert, Baraguey and Delmas, 18,500 men, constituted the left wing in the vicinity of Trent; Baraguey was at the head of the Brenta valley. The divisions of Massena, Guieu, Serurier and Bernadotte, 43,000 men, constituted the right wing. Massena was at Bassano, Guieu at Castelfranco, Serurier near Castelfranco and Bernadotte at Padua. About 2,000 men were left on the Adige and 1,500 in Mantua.

Although Mantua had surrendered, the Austrian government was still unwilling to make peace and again sought to strengthen its army in Italy. Alvinczi was relieved from command at his own request and Archduke Charles, who had been successful in Germany, was sent to relieve him. The Archduke first visited the Tyrol and reached Italy just as Napoleon was about to open the campaign. He found the Austrian troops disorganized and morally weakened by their many defeats. He decided that it was impossible to attempt more than the defence of the frontier, until he could receive reinforcements and reorganize his army. Leaving a brigade on the lower Brenta to watch the crossings and a brigade at Feltre to guard the mountain road connecting the Piave and Drave valleys, he withdrew his main body behind the Tagliamento to reorganize.

At this time the Austrian troops on the Tagliamento were organized into six brigades of about 4,000 men each. To protect his communications with Vienna there were two small brigades of perhaps 1,500 to 2,000 each in the gorge of the Tagliamento south of Pontafel (Pontebba), and in the gorge of the Isonzo south of Tarvis. It was believed by the Archduke that both of these detachments would be strongly reinforced by detachments coming from Vienna before the French could reach them.

The Archduke did not feel strong enough to resist Napoleon, for whose abilities he had great respect, but decided to remain on the Tagliamento and retard the French troops as much as possible. He had already decided on his plan of retreat, which was to be towards Triest; possibly because Napoleon had threatened to destroy that port, and possibly to compel Napoleon to follow a longer route than the direct route to Vienna through Tarvis and thus give more time for the Austrian reinforcements to reach that point.

*Campaign.—March 10.—*On March 10, Massena opened the campaign by moving up the Brenta valley to Primolano and thence over the mountains to Feltre. On the following days he pursued the Austrian brigade which had been at Feltre beyond the town of Belluno and captured the commander and a fifth of his brigade.

The other three divisions crossed the Piave without opposition on the Treviso road on the 12th, and on the 15th were on the Tagliamento. From Belluno, Massena was ordered to cross the mountains to the Tagliamento but was unable to do so. He was compelled to move southward to the plain and thence to the Tagliamento, arriving there on the 17th.

*March 16.—*Without waiting for Massena's arrival, the other three divisions crossed the Tagliamento, which happened to be low and fordable. After a short resistance, the Austrian army retreated as previously planned—5,000 men under Gen. Bajalich with the army trains took the road for Tarvis *via* Udine and Caporetto, while the Archduke with the remainder of his army retreated towards the Isonzo at Gorz and Gradisca.

*March 17.—*Napoleon now decided to seize the direct road to Vienna and ordered Massena, who had joined him, to march up the Tagliamento valley and seize Tarvis. In order that Joubert might join him there, orders were sent Joubert to advance *via* Botzen to Brixen whence a road ran eastward through the Drave valley to Villach.

Bernadotte, Serurier and Guieu were ordered to follow the Archduke towards Triest.

*March 19.—*Massena forced the gorge of the Tagliamento 18 miles south of Pontafel held by 2,000 Austrians. Bernadotte and Serurier captured the fortified town of Gradisca with its garrison of one brigade. Guieu was on the Udine-Gorz road to their north.

March 20.—Massena entered Pontafel without opposition. Bernadotte and Serurier marched on Gorz by the east bank of the Isonzo while Guieu moved northward to enter the Isonzo valley at Caporetto and join Massena at Tarvis.

March 21.—Massena's advance guard reached Tarvis 22 miles from Pontafel and drove out a small Austrian garrison but was in turn driven out by the advance guard of the Austrian column moving up the Isonzo escorting the Austrian army trains.

Napoleon remained at Gorz while Bernadotte and Serurier moved on the road towards Laibach. The reserve cavalry brigade moved to Triest to take possession of that port.

March 22.—Massena recaptured Tarvis early in the morning and prevented the exit from the Isonzo valley of one-half of Bajalich's column. Guieu was moving up the Isonzo valley from Caporetto.

March 23.—Bajalich's force in the Isonzo valley caught between Massena and Guieu surrendered with the army train of 30 guns and 400 wagons.

March 25.—Gen. Serurier being too ill to command his division, it fell to Gen. Chabot who was ordered to move up the Isonzo valley to Tarvis.

March 26.—Napoleon had remained at Gorz from the 21st to the 26th to organize a government. On the 26th he turned over the government to Bernadotte and started for Tarvis.

March 28.—Napoleon reached Tarvis and pushed on to Villach where he found most of his troops. At this time Joubert was at Brixen, with Delmas' division at Botzen. The Archduke was at Klagenfurt, where a part of his troops from Laibach and reinforcements from Vienna had joined him. These added to the troops defeated by Massena gave him a force of 13,000 to 14,000 men.

March 29 to April 17.—The divisions of Massena, Guieu and Chabot moved out from Villach March 29, and pursued the Austrian forces as far as Leoben. There were several rear guard actions in the mountain passes.

On April 7, Napoleon was at Judenburg 150 miles from Vienna, and his advance guard at Leoben, 116 miles from that capital. Bernadotte had joined him *via* Laibach and Klagenfurt.

On the 31st of March, Napoleon had written to the Archduke

suggesting peace; and on April 7, an armistice was arranged between the military commanders. This practically ended the campaign of less than one month..

On April 17, an agreement was signed by the representatives of the two governments providing for the termination of hostilities and a peace conference.

While Napoleon was advancing from the Tagliamento, Joubert, in accordance with his orders, advanced through Botzen to Brixen where he waited for further orders. He left a division at Botzen and a detachment at Trent.

The Austrians now began to attack him and he was placed in an embarrassing position by the concentration of a superior Austrian force in front of Botzen, which threatened his communications.

He was relieved from his embarrassment by the arrival of a French officer in disguise, who had made his way from Villach. Joubert at once, April 3, called in the division from Botzen and started for Villach April 5, 140 miles distant.

On April 10, he reached Spital—24 miles from Villach—where he met a French force sent by Napoleon, and learned of the armistice.

After the signing of the armistice between the two governments, Massena was sent to Paris to present it to the government and the French army withdrew from Austrian territory.

NAPOLEON'S COMMENTS.

1. The Archduke, desiring to cover Vienna and Triest, should have united his forces in the Tyrol, where the inhabitants and the topography of the country would have assisted him and where he could easily receive assistance from the Austrian army on the Rhine. As long as he maintained himself in the Tyrol, he had no reason to fear a French advance beyond the Isonzo. If the French general advanced eastward from the Piave, the Archduke could advance along the Adige; this would compel the French general to concentrate to meet this movement. A successful movement by the French against the Archduke in the Tyrol would have been .extremely difficult.

2. The Archduke, in taking up his position on the Tagliamento, should have adopted the road up the Tagliamento as his line of retreat. It should have been evident to him that Napoleon was planning to seize Tarvis.

3. After the fight on the Tagliamento, it was a mistake for him to send any troops towards Tarvis, as it was almost certain that Massena

would reach there first. It was equally useless for him to leave any troops at Gradisca after marching his main force to the rear. These troops were only sacrificed.

4. Was not the march of the French army by its two lines of operation contrary to the principle that an army should have but one line of operations? Was not the uniting of these two columns near Villach in violation of the principle never to unite columns in front of or near the enemy? Would it not have been better to have given Napoleon 10,000 more, and Joubert 10,000 less, and ordered the latter to act strictly on the defensive? By this plan, war in the Tyrol, a difficult field of operations, would have been avoided; the dangers attending a concerted movement would also have been avoided, and at the outset, all the troops would have been concentrated.

None of the above principles was violated. It would have been very unwise to have left Joubert with a small force and made it possible for the Austrians to drive him back and reach Verona before the French reached Villach. It was wiser to make him strong enough to assume the offensive and drive the Austrians over the Brenner pass.

We did not enter Austria by two lines, since the road from Trent to Villach, *via* Botzen and Brixen, is on the south side of the main chain of the Alps. Joubert made no movement imtil the Tagliamento was crossed and the possession of Tarvis was assured. After that, it was impossible for the Archduke to so manoeuvre as to prevent the union of the two wings of the army.

FRENCH GENERALS OF DIVISION.

Baraguey-d'Hilliers, Louis.—Born 1764. Entered army in 1783 as cadet, lieut. colonel 1787, general of brigade 1793, general of division 1797. Served in the Army of the Rhine, in the Army of Italy in 1797, in Egypt 1798, in the Army of the Rhine in 1800, in the campaign of Austerlitz. in 1808-1809- 1810 in Italy, in 1812 in Russia. Died in Berlin 1812.

Bernadotte, Charles Jean.—Born in France 1764. Enlisted in the army in 1781, sergeant 1789, chief of battalion of volunteers 1792, general of brigade 1793, general of division 1794, minister of war 1799, marshal 1804. Served along the Rhine in the early part of French Revolution, joined the Army of Italy in 1797. As commander of the 1st army corps took part in the campaigns of Austerlitz, Jena, Eylau and Friedland 1805-1807. In 1810 was elected by the Swedish states to succeed Charles XIII and as Prince Royal engaged with the allies in the campaigns of 1813-1814 against France. Under the French empire he was made Prince of Ponte Corvo, became king of Sweden in 1818 as Charles XIV. Died 1844.

Chabot, Louis Jean.—Born 1764. Entered army 1754, captain 1792, general of brigade 1793, general of division 1795. Served in the Army of the West, commanded a division of the besieging army at Mantua when Wurmser surrendered, served in Spain 1808 and 1809, joined the Bourbons in 1814 and did not return to Napoleon in 1815. Died 1837.

Delmas, Antoine Guillaume.—Entered army in 1780, chief of battalion 1891, general of brigade 1793, general of division 1793. Served in the Army of the Rhine, served in the Army of Italy in 1797. Under the Empire he was relieved from command because he was a friend of Gen. Moreau but later was restored.—Fatally wounded at Leipsic 1813.

Dumas, Thomas Alexander.—Born 1762 in San Domingo. Entered army in 1786, lieut. colonel of cavalry 1789, general of brigade 1793, general of division 1793. Served in the Army of the West, in the Army of Italy in 1797, in Egypt in 1798, captured on his return voyage and imprisoned in Naples for two years. On his return to France he was opposed to Napoleon as First Consul and relieved from command. Died 1806. Father of Alexander Dumas.

Guieu, Jean Joseph.—Born 1758. Enlisted in artillery in 1780, chief of battalion 1792, chief of brigade and general of brigade 1793, general of division 1797, retired 1798, died 1817. His principal service was with the Army of Italy in the divisions of Sauret, Vaubois and Augereau.

Victor, Claude.—Born 1764. Entered the army as drummer in 1781 and served until 1789. Entered the volunteers as a private in 1792, chief of battalion in 1793, and general of brigade for conduct in siege of Toulon in 1793, general of division in 1796, marshal in 1807. He served in the Army of the Pyrenees 1793-5, in that of Italy 1796-7 and in 1799, in the Reserve Army 1800, temporarily commander of the 1st and 10th corps in 1807 and as commander of former participated in the battle of Friedland; served with distinction in Spain 1809, took an active part in the campaign of Moscow and in those of 1813 and 1814 which followed it. Upon Napoleon's abdication he offered his services to Louis XVIII. and retired from France during the Hundred Days. He was afterwards minister of war, but retired from public service after the revolution of 1830. He died in 1841. During the Empire he was made Duke of Belluno.

AUSTRIAN ARMY COMMANDER.

Charles, Ludwig, Archduke of Austria.—Born 1771. In 1792-1794 took an active part in campaigns and battles of Jemappes, Aldenhoven, Neerwinden, Landrecies, Tournay, Courtray and Fleurus. In 1796 commander of Army of Rhine drove Jourdan and Moreau across Rhine and captured Kehl. In 1797 commander of Italian army. In 1799 commander Rhine army and defeated Jourdan in four battles. Commander of Italian Army in 1805, and of the Austrian army on the Danube 1809. Defeated by Napoleon in the campaigns of 1797 and 1809.

ARMY OF ITALY—MARCH 5, 1797.

Right Wing—Napoleon.

Division	Brigade	Demi-brigades	Strength
	Motte	2nd Light	
Massena	Menard	18th Line	11,000
	Brune	20th "	
	Rampon	25th "	
		32nd "	
	LeClerc	10th Chasseurs	
		3rd Dragoons	
	Point	27th Light	
Augereau	Verdier	4th Line	
Guieu	Bon	40th "	
	Lafont	43rd "	
		51st "	10,800
	Davin	21st Light	
	Charton	12th Line	
Serurier	Meyer	64th "	
Chabot		69th "	9,600
		6th "	
	Beaumont	25th Chasseurs	
	Fiorella	15th Light	
	Friant	30th Line	
	Chabran	55th "	
Bernadotte		61st "	9,900
		88th "	

	Murat	4th Chasseurs	
		14th Dragoons	
Cavalry reserve	Dugua	1st Hussars	1,100
	Walther	24th Chasseurs	
		9th Dragoons	
		5th Cavalry	
Artillery and engineers			1,600

Total, right wing,	43,000

Left Wing—Joubert.

		4th Light	
	Pelletire	17th "	
	Vial	22nd "	
	Monnier	29th "	7,000
Joubert	Belliard	14th Line	
	Vaud	18th "	
	David	33rd "	
	Serviez	68th "	
		85th "	
	Vergez	11th Light	
Baraguay	Chevalier	12th "	5,500
		39th Line	
		58th "	
	Pijon	26th Light	
Delmas	Vavay	5th Line	4,500
	Dufresse	93rd "	
Artillery and engineers			500
Dumas (cavalry reserve)		22nd Chasseurs	1,000
		5th Dragoons	
		8th "	

Total, left wing,	18,500
Total force,	61,500

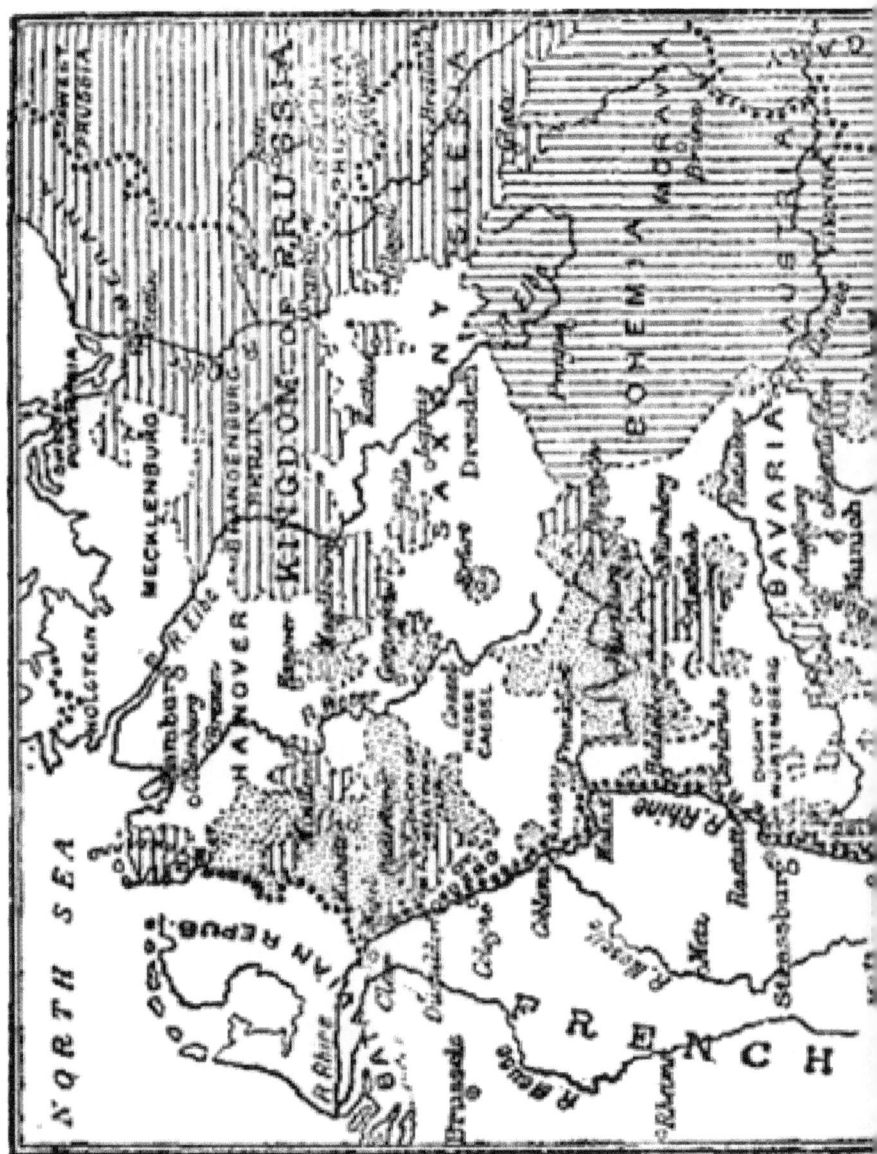

AUSTRIAN DOMINIONS
SWISS CONFEDERATION
Bern
Zurich
Constance
Geneva
PIEDMONT
Turin
R. Po
Milan
Parma
Bologna
CISALPINE
REPUB.
LIGURIAN REPUB.
Venice
VENICE
CARNIOLA
TURKEY
ADRIATIC SEA
Rimini
Ancona
Tolentino
Leghorn
TUSCANY
STATES OF THE CHURCH
ROME
R. Tiber
PARTHENOPEAN REP.
Capua
Elba
CORSICA
Ajaccio
SARDINIA
MEDITERRANEAN SEA
Avignon
Marseille
Toulon
Nice
Lyon
R. Rhone
R. Doubs
Scale of Miles
0
50
100

Organization of the Army of Italy

Infantry.—In 1794, the two-battalion regiments of the regular French army were abolished by the following decree:—

The infantry shall be formed into *demi*-brigades, each containing one of the battalions of the former regiments of the line (regulars) and two battalions of volunteers (of 1792 and 1793). The *demi*-brigade shall have 2,437 men and six 4-pounder guns.

One hundred and forty *demi*-brigades were authorized.

As the troops were in active campaign, this transformation took time, and all the battalions were not incorporated in *demi*-brigades when Napoleon took command of the Army of Italy. There was also confusion in numbering the *demi*-brigades and many of those in the army had their number changed during the campaign.

The *demi*-brigade was commanded by a *chef de brigade* (colonel) who was assisted by a junior *chef de brigade* (lieutenant colonel).

Each battalion was commanded by a *chef de bataillon* (major) and was composed of nine companies with four officers each.

The infantry was of two classes—*infantry of the line* and *light infantry*. About one-fourth of the *demi*-brigades were light infantry.

Each battalion had nine companies of which one was an elite company whose officers and men were selected and received higher pay than those of like rank in the other companies. That of the line battalions was called the *grenadier* company and that of the light infantry the *carabinier* company. These companies did not fight in line or column with the other companies, but were reserved for special tasks.

The line infantry formed the line of battle and against infantry employed the bayonet in attack and the musket in defence. The light infantry was for skirmishing and mountain warfare and relied principally on fire action and on rapid marching.

One of the changes made by Napoleon in the infantry during his Italian operations was to arm with muskets the lieutenants and sergeants of the light infantry and the sergeants of line infantry, who had formerly carried swords. Another was to give rifles to the *carabinier* companies of the light infantry.

Napoleon was a strict advocate of the bayonet. He fixed a fine for the loss of the bayonet, which was to be expended in purchasing new ones. "The bayonet has always been the arm of the brave man and the principal instrument of victory. It is the arm best suited to the French soldier."

Of the many infantry officers, who afterwards rose to higher rank, the most conspicuous was Lannes who began as *chef de bataillon* and for his conspicuous bravery, rose to general of brigade in these campaigns. Rampon rose from *chef de brigade* to general of brigade for his defence of Monte Legino.

Cavalry.—The cavalry of the French army was composed of regiments of cavalry, hussars, dragoons and *chasseurs*—86 in all. The cavalry regiments were of the *cuirrassier* class, intended for the battlefield; the hussars were the light cavalry for outpost duty against cavalry; the dragoons were analogous to the line infantry having carbines with bayonets; the *chasseurs* were analogous to the light infantry and carried the carbine without bayonets.

All the cavalry was formed into regiments of four squadrons of 160 men each.

When Napoleon took command of the army, his cavalry consisted of eleven regiments:—2 of hussars, 5 of *chasseurs* and 4 of dragoons. Two or more regiments formed a brigade. At the beginning of his operations he formed them into two divisions, but after the death of General Stengel he formed them into brigades of which one was always in reserve and the others were attached to the infantry divisions.

He also organized the *guides*, his own personal escort, which in these campaigns was only a squadron. The guides were later employed in his Egyptian campaign, and then became the nucleus of the consular and imperial guard.

Until Napoleon took command, all the operations of the Army of Italy had taken place in the mountains, where cavalry was difficult to maintain and where it had a limited field of action. Napoleon at first distrusted its field and regimental officers because of their limited experience, and wrote at once for three young adjutants-general, who had seen service in the cavalry, been under fire, and were resolved not to make skilful retreats. These were to serve on the staff of the chief of cavalry.

He also applied at once for horse artillery, which had been introduced into the French service in 1792, as he did not care to expose his cavalry to the Austrian cavalry without the support of this auxiliary arm.

The most conspicuous service performed by the cavalry was its reconnaissance work, for which it was especially suited.

Some of the most skilful cavalry leaders of the Napoleonic era had their first lessons of real warfare in these campaigns.

Murat became brigadier general when Stengel was killed. Bessieres had command of the guides. Lasalle won his first important advancement at Rivoli.

Of the cavalry officers of the old royal army, Gens. Stengel,. Dumas and Beaumont served with distinction.

Artillery.—In 1796 the French army had eight regular regiments of light and siege artillery of twenty companies each, and eight regular regiments of horse artillery of nine companies each. Each *demi*-brigade of infantry was expected to have six light guns, two to a battalion, managed by a company of volunteer artillery.

The Army of Italy had in 1796 very little effective light artillery and no horse artillery.

In the French army at this time, the horses and drivers of the artillery were furnished and maintained by contractors, or the horses were purchased and the men hired by the supply department of the army, as in our own wagon and pack trains. They did not belong to the artillery proper.

The Army of Italy was very weak in transportation and fought its first battles largely with the *demi*-brigade light guns, probably drawn by the troops.

After the French captured Lodi, Napoleon established his artillery depot there and began the organization of his field artillery..

For his advance on the Mincio in May, he was able to furnish each of his four infantry divisions with a light battery of six guns and his cavalry with a similar battery. The pieces were 3-pounders, 5-pounders, 8-pounders and field howitzers. To secure drivers he called on each of his infantry divisions for 100 men. The horses were obtained by requisition.

He continued to improve this arm and in the spring of 1797, its organization was as follows:—

Each infantry division had two batteries of artillery; one battery was light artillery, and the other horse or mountain, depending upon its field of operations.

The battery, or *division* as it was called, was composed of six guns and six caissons. Because of the variety of pieces in the army, one platoon in each battery had 3-, 4-, or 5-pounders, another 11- or 12-pounders, and the third howitzers. The personnel of each battery consisted of 72 cannoneers, of whom 32 belonged to some regular artillery company and the remainder to some volunteer company. The remaining men of the two companies from whom these were drawn were attached to the artillery park.

The drivers and horses of the battery formed a distinct organization, called a *train brigade* under the charge of a *conducteur* and were also divided into three platoons. Two inspectors supervised the artillery trains of the army.

Besides these divisional batteries, he organized as many similar batteries for an artillery reserve as possible.

Under his chief of artillery there was an assistant chief in charge of the field, and one of the siege artillery.

His most efficient artillery officer was General Lespinasse who rose under him from colonel to general of division for his service in the Army of Italy. He was at the time sixty years old and had had a high reputation in his corps. Napoleon said of him "He was one of those generals of artillery who love best to be with the advance guard."

Of the younger officers of artillery who later became famous, the most conspicuous was Marmont, who was lieutenant and *aide* of Napoleon and rose to *chef de brigade* during the campaigns. He was frequently intrusted by Napoleon with placing the artillery in position on the battlefield.

The *pontoniers*, who then formed a branch of the artillery, were under Gen. Andreossy (1761-1828) who joined the Army of Italy as a *chef de bataillon* in the artillery. As Napoleon had no bridge train before Lodi, it was Andreossy who organized this branch of the service engaging sailors for this purpose. He also organized flotillas on Lake Garda and on the lakes around Mantua.

When Napoleon entered the campaign against Archduke Charles he had two complete bridge trains with the army besides a number of floating bridges across the rivers on his lines of communication.

For his service in the Army of Italy, Andreossy was promoted to general of brigade.

Engineers.—At the outbreak of the French revolution the French corps of engineers consisted only of a corps of officers. In 1794 the six battalions of miners and twelve battalions of sappers were transferred from the artillery to the engineers.

When Napoleon took command, there were small detachments of both miners and sappers but without proper organization. His first step was to organize a strong company of engineer troops capable of performing all kinds of technical work.

Having no officers educated at the engineer school of Mezieres, Colonel Chasseloup (1754-1833), one of the most distinguished engineers in the army, was sent him. He took charge of siege operations at Milan and Mantua and reconstructed the fortifications of Verona, Legnago, Peschiera, Padua and many other Italian cities. He acted with Lespinasse in fortifying the lines of the covering army of Mantua and with Andreossy in establishing and defending the bridges.

For his services at Mantua he was promoted to general of brigade and later to general of division.

"He was one of the best officers of his corps; of uneven character but with a complete knowledge of all the resources of his art."— Napoleon at St. Helena.

Napoleon formed small pioneer detachments in each battalion of infantry by equipping four men with axes, two with spades and two with picks. Bayonets were attached to the handles of these tools for defence.

Brigade.—Two *demi*-brigades of infantry formed a brigade commanded by a general of brigade. The number of generals of brigades usually exceeded the number of brigades and it was a common custom for generals of brigade to lead a *demi*-brigade in battle, or command it on the march.

Division.—The infantry division of the French army was, like the infantry division of to-day, a complete unit with all arms. The composition of the division both in infantry and cavalry was changed to meet the requirements of the duty it was directed to perform. It was commanded by a general of division, who was assisted by several adjutants-general.

In the course of his operations Napoleon established a base for each infantry division and for his cavalry, in the cities between the Mincio and Ticino Rivers. Officers and men reporting from sick leave or the hospitals, recruits and general supplies, were sent to these bases, thus reducing the confusion at the front.

The General Staff.—The general staff of the army consisted of a chief of staff and a number of adjutants-general assigned as chief of staff of divisions, or simply as aids to these chiefs of staff. They had the rank of *chef de brigade* or *chef de bataillon.* They had charge of the military correspondence, reports, reconnaissance work, map making, inspections, etc. They frequently led columns in battle and several of them became generals of brigade.

Supply.—The supply of the armies was by contract. All officials of the supply and pay departments were civilians and had no military status. The officials of this department were both inefficient and corrupt, and as Napoleon states, made the expense of the army about five times what it should have been, besides reducing its efficiency by irregularity in supplying food, forage and pay; notwithstanding the heavy requisitions made upon the country in which he was operating. Napoleon struggled in vain to correct the abuses of this department by discharging and imprisoning its employees. They requisitioned without authority and sold the supplies belonging to the government and the army for their own benefit.

French System of Tactics.

The normal formation of the *line infantry* was in three ranks and in two lines.

In the attack, the battalions were in mass with a two-company front and a depth of twelve men. The interval between battalion columns was that of six companies in line. In defence, the battalions of the first line were in line, the third rank forming local reserves. The battalions of the second line were in mass.

The normal formation of the *light infantry* was in two ranks.

In the attack, the light infantry was deployed in front of the line battalions, forming a skirmish line with yard intervals.

Firing as they advanced, they concealed the line battalions by a cloud of smoke and when they arrived at fifty yards from the enemy they gathered in the intervals between the line battalions and kept up their fire to cover the attack or permit the withdrawal of the line troops.

The line battalions advanced steadily at an ordinary pace—the leading companies with guns at the charge and the others at the shoulder—until the enemy's line was reached, when the rear companies rushed up to carry the point of the enemy's line in front of the battalion with fixed bayonets.

The second line advanced about 250 yards in rear of the first to reinforce its attack.

The grenadiers marched on the flank of the battalion to protect it from flank attack and the cavalry was on the flanks to guard the whole from flank attacks by the enemy's cavalry. If not successfully protected by cavalry, the battalions halted and formed squares until the enemy's cavalry was driven off.

The battalion guns were placed in the intervals between battalions and advanced with the light infantry.

Napoleon did not follow blindly any system of tactics. At Arcole, which was a fight of the heads of columns, Napoleon placed his grenadiers in front of each column. He usually massed his guns on what he considered the key points of the enemy's line. Thus, at Castiglione, he placed 20 guns in a single battery under Marmont; these largely contributed to his victory.

DISCIPLINE IN THE ARMY OF ITALY.

When Napoleon took command of the Army of Italy at Nice, he issued the following circular March 27, 1796.

Soldiers, you are naked, and starving; the government owes you much and can give you nothing. The patience and the courage you show amongst these rocks are admirable, but no glory, not even a ray, can shine upon you. I am going to lead you into the most fertile plains of the world. Rich provinces, great cities will be in your power; there you will find honour, glory and riches. Soldiers of Italy, will your courage or your perseverance fail?

The picture he drew of the condition of the Army of Italy was not overdrawn. The division commanders were petitioning for shoes, at least for the men on outpost duty in the mountains. Serurier reported that his men went on raiding expeditions without orders and would rather raid than fight. One artillery company had sold its cannon, for the purpose of getting food. Massena reported his men dying of scurvy. Laharpe reported his men as rebellious and saying they would fight in the same manner as they were paid. Napoleon himself had to disband a battalion at Nice that refused to march to the front until they were paid. Massena reported the advance guard as in need of two thousand muskets.

Napoleon concealed neither from his soldiers nor from himself the fact that the only hope for that army lay in an advance movement. He praised the courage and patience of the men and refrained from saying anything about their insubordination, for he hoped to conquer that by supplying their physical wants. He therefore spent the days preceding operations in personally organizing pack trains to supply the men and in forwarding such supplies as he had been able to procure.

He trusted to the reputation he had made at Toulon and in 1794, and to their desire to relieve their bodily wants, to carry them forward when the time came.

The first town they captured was Dego which they promptly began to loot; they were surprised by the Austrians and driven from it. On the Corsaglia, Serurier's men captured the village of St. Michael, and at once began to loot it; this compelled Serurier to retreat. Before the battle of Mondovi was over, the French troops began to loot and almost lost the battle.

After the battle of Mondovi, Napoleon issued an order on the subject of looting, containing the following extracts:—

The general in chief expresses to the army his satisfaction with the bravery of his troops and their daily victories over their adversaries; but he witnesses with horror the frightful pillage of the perverse men who join their organization only after the battle and deliver themselves to excesses which dishonour the army and the nation.

Generals of division are authorized to relieve and to send to Antibes in arrest the officers who have by their example authorized the horrible pillage of the last few days.

The generals of division are authorized, according to circumstances, to have shot at once, officers or soldiers who by their example incite others to pillage and by it destroy discipline, thus bringing the army into disorder and compromising its safety and glory.

Every officer and non-commissioned officer who has not followed his colours and is absent from a combat without authority will be at once relieved, and his name will be sent to his department in France, where he will be posted as a coward.

Every soldier who is twice convicted of skulking, will be published in orders to his battalion.

Every soldier deserting his colours will lose his seniority and be placed at the foot of his company. If he belongs to the grenadiers or *carabiniers* his name will be erased from the company roll. Any soldier twice convicted of cowardice will be degraded before his battalion and sent beyond the Var to work on the roads during the campaign.

Generals of division, generals of brigade and commanding officers will be held responsible for the execution of this order.

Notwithstanding this order, pillage and looting continued to the end of the campaign of 1797, although it was much restricted when the army was in Austria, where Napoleon wished to win the good will of the inhabitants. Much of the looting was due to the defective supply system of the army, which failed to furnish rations, forage or pay with any regularity, and also to the policy of the French government which not only requisitioned supplies in Italy, but robbed its museums of its choicest works of art.

It is natural that the volunteers raised during the Reign of Terror in France, when liberty and license were almost synonymous terms, should be difficult to bring under the restraint of military order. In this respect the officers were as bad as the men, as may be judged from the following extract:—

January 1797.

Direct General Lannes to depart two hours after the receipt of this order to join the 19th *demi*-brigade at Borgo San Donino and march at its head. Order every officer to march with his command, and the *demi*-brigade to keep closed up. All the officers must be with their companies and not riding in carriages. Let the *demi*-brigade have the appearance of belonging to the Army of Italy, and not to the king of Persia.

You will direct General Lannes to relieve the first officer who rides in a carriage and is not with his company, in accordance with this order.

He will assemble the officers on his arrival and inform them that I am displeased with their disorder on the march.

It must be remembered that this order was issued towards the end of his operations and that General Lannes was one of his best officers. It should be said however that the 19th *demi*-brigade had been doing fortress work until this time.

Napoleon was fortunate in his division commanders, as far as military operations were concerned, but they did not all assist him in establishing discipline. Of Massena he says, "He neglected discipline, was careless about administration, and was not liked by his men." As a matter of fact the company officers of the Army of Rome, to which he was assigned after this campaign, and which included his own division and one other, had a meeting in the Pantheon and relieved him from command; a step which the Directory felt compelled to approve.

Augereau was popular with his men, as he was a violent republican and treated his men as companions and equals. It is doubtful if his command was well disciplined.

Serurier was an officer of the old army and never got over his distrust of the volunteers, who could not be brought under the same discipline as his old regulars. He was not therefore popular with his command. Laharpe, being a strong republican and having sacrificed his personal interests for France, was well liked.

Sauret and Vaubois had not the strength of character necessary for disciplinarians of a volunteer command.

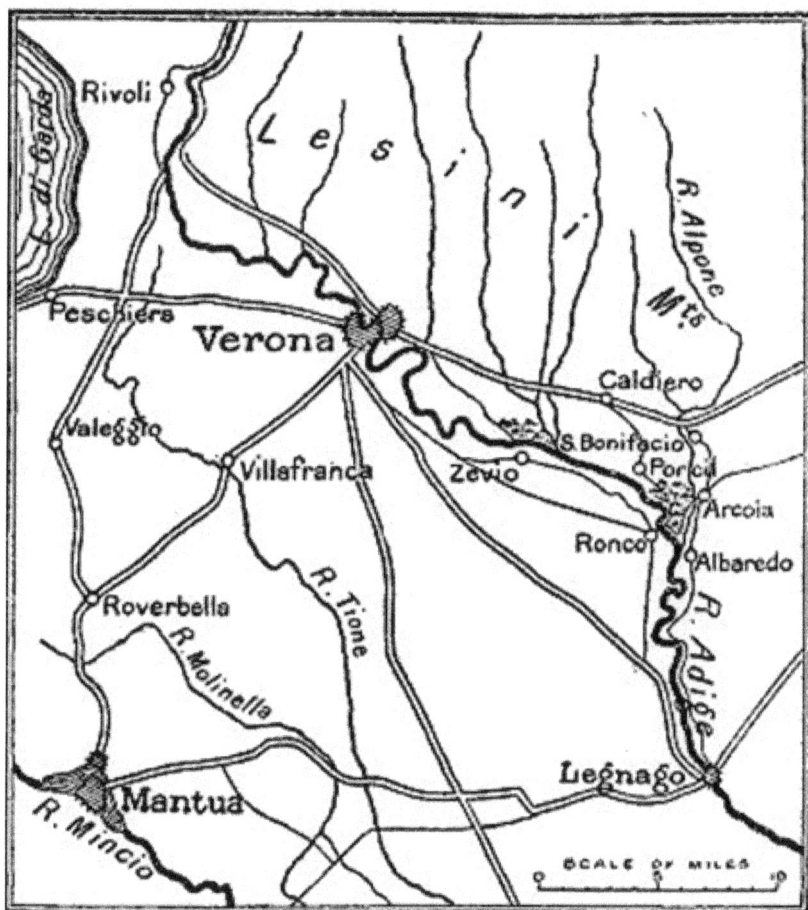

PLAN TO ILLUSTRATE THE VICTORY OF ARCOLA

Some of the Causes
of Napoleon's Success

1. *The morale of his army.*—Unlike Massena, Napoleon sought the goodwill and confidence of his soldiers; and unlike Serurier he trusted them. He sought to make them proud of their army, of their military unit, and of their personal reputation.

On the 24th of April, 1796, immediately after the battle of Mondovi, he sent his *aide*—Junot—with twenty-one colours captured in the Battles of Montenotte, Millesimo, Dego and Mondovi, to Paris, to present them with ceremony to the Directory.

In his letter of transmittal, to be read to the Directors, he says, "The Army of Italy in presenting you with these twenty-one colours, testimonials of its bravery, charges me to assure you of its devotion to the constitution and to the magistrates (the directors), etc."

After each important victory a similar messenger was sent to impress upon France and the world the feats of the Army of Italy and to make every individual in that army proud of its name.

To make officers and soldiers take pride in their organizations he had inscribed on the colours of the battalions the engagements in which they took part; those in which they played an important part, were inscribed in larger letters than the others. On the colours of the 57th *demi*-brigade he had inscribed, "The terrible 57th which nothing can resist"; on those of two *demi*-brigades of Vaubois' division, who had shown demoralization in the retreat from Trent, he had inscribed, "This battalion is not of the Army of Italy."

After each engagement he promptly made a report to Paris, and in it mentioned the organizations that played an important part in it and described the feats performed by them.

To encourage individual officers and men, promotion promptly followed any conspicuous act. Rampon was appointed brevet general four days after Montenotte and recommended for promotion to the War Department. Lanusse and Lannes were promoted immediately after the Battle of Dego in which they had played conspicuous parts.

After every engagement the commanding generals were directed to report the names of officers and men who had distinguished themselves, and they were promptly promoted if their previous record had been good.

Besides promotion. Napoleon rewarded individuals by presenting officers with swords of honour and the men with muskets of honour, and by making grants of money from that obtained by requisition or by the sale of captured stores. A soldier who captured a horse from the enemy's army was allowed to turn it in and draw its value in money.

2. *His military instinct.*—He had a faculty for correctly estimating a military situation, whether it was limited to a battlefield, or extended over a theatre of war.

While Massena was worrying over the exposed situation of the brigade at Voltri in the early days of April 1796, it gave Napoleon no concern. He realized at once that Beaulieu could not alone advance on Savona along the coast; Savona was in danger only from an attack *via* Montenotte or Cairo. He therefore sent Marmont to Voltri to estimate Beaulieu's strength and withdraw the French brigade, while he remained near Savona to prepare his counter movement.

The turning movement *via* Piacenza, the campaigns against Wurmser and Alvinczi, all show this faculty of grasping the weakness in an enemy's general dispositions. At Rivoli was shown his ability to select the key point of a battlefield.

His mind acted as clearly when the enemy seemed to have him at a disadvantage, as in the first campaigns of Wurmser and Alvinczi, as it did when he had the enemy at a disadvantage, as in his campaign against Beaulieu and his second campaign against Wurmser.

He apparently failed to grasp the military situation in the summer of 1796, when he allowed Wurmser to surprise him. This was due to the fact that he had probably been misinformed as to the character of the country west of Lake Garda, and because he was obliged to go to Mantua and trust Massena to dispose his troops to the best advantage to cover Mantua.

In his first campaign against Alvinczi, he was deceived as to the character of Alvinczi's troops, by some prisoners taken by Massena. The latter reported them as very inferior soldiers.

3. *His ability to make prompt decisions and act in accordance with them.*—
While many generals fail because they cannot correctly estimate a
military situation, quite as many more fail because they cannot decide
to act promptly in accordance with their estimate. Napoleon appreci-
ated the value of time.

From the moment a campaign opened until it closed, the French
troops were in motion with a definite purpose, almost continuously.
As they realized that they were marching with an object, they could
accomplish feats that would have been impossible for troops who had
less confidence in their commander.

It was his ability to make prompt decisions and act upon them,
that enabled him to unite his divisions and attack those of his enemy
in detail.

Few generals, without a bridge train, would have conceived the
idea of crossing a river like the Po in hostile territory, or, if they did
conceive it, would have dared to risk laurels won at Montenotte, Dego,
Millessimo and Mondovi, in such an operation.

Few generals would have been able to make up their minds to
abandon the siege of Mantua to attack Wurmser's field army, until it
was too late. Napoleon had had great difficulty in getting together
enough siege artillery to attack the place and he knew that if this
artillery was now abandoned it could not be replaced. He must then
resort to investment and give the Austrians the opportunity of sending
relieving armies to raise the siege.

His decision to attack Alvinczi's communications *via* Arcole was his
most remarkable conception, and his decision to persist in it notwithstanding his lack of success on the first day, by withdrawing additional
troops from Vaubois' depleted and demoralized command, was even
more remarkable. It is safe to say no other general of history would
have been capable of the conception and execution of this plan.

4. *His aggressiveness.*—Throughout the campaign he showed a desire to bring matters to an issue as soon as possible.

5. *His indifference to physical danger.*—He never hesitated to expose
himself if it seemed desirable.

He impressed his officers and men with the fact that honour and
promotion were only for those who led the way in an attack.

6. *His calmness and self control in all situations.*—He was never duly
elated by victory or unduly depressed by defeat. When he was surrounded by a superior force of Austrians at Lonato in August 1796,

and the Austrian commander sent an aide with a flag of truce to demand the surrender of the place, Napoleon had the *aide* brought into his presence blindfolded and removed his bandage in the presence of himself and staff. He then upbraided him for his audacity in demanding the surrender of a general-in-chief in the midst of his army, and sent him back with a demand for the immediate surrender of the Austrian force. The Austrian force surrendered.

His calmness on the battlefield enabled him to observe the progress of a battle and employ his troops to the best advantage. It also enabled him to observe the conduct of individuals, to make every officer and soldier feel that the eyes of the general commanding was upon him and he would be rewarded or punished, according to his conduct.

7. *His indefatigable energy.*—Although slight in person. Napoleon was at this time in fine physical condition and could stand both great mental and physical effort. His active mind allowed no rest for himself, his generals, or his army while there remained anything to be done. When not in active campaign he was constantly employed on political missions and in reorganizing his army. This energy caused him to weed out from his army every officer who was sluggish, mentally or physically, and retain only those who had his own activity.

NORTHERN ITALY

ILLUSTRATING

THE CAMPAIGNS OF

1796 AND 1797

STATUTE MILES

0   10   20   30   40   50   60

ADRIATIC SEA

GULF OF VENICE

MEDITERRANEAN SEA

GULF OF GENOA

SWITZERLAND

AUSTRIA

TYROL

SARDINIA

TUSCANY

LOMBARDY

VENICE

MODENA

PARMA

LUCCA

GENOA

FRANCE

Udine

Car po-Formio

Belluno

Coneglilano

Trevi

Primolano

Bassano

VENICE

Trent

Neumarkt

Roveredo

Mte. Baldo

Vicenza

Lonigo

Padua

Rovigo

Verona

Montebello

Caldiero

Ronco

Arcole

Legnago

Ferrara

Bologna

Ravenna

Faenza

S.Magno

Rimini

Pesaro

GW.Colton.N.Y.

Salo

Corona

Rivoli

Brescia

Desenzano

Castiglione

Goito

Volta

Lonato

Bergamo

Solferino

Mantua

Reggio

Modena

Carpi

Brescello

STATES OF THE CHURCH

Chiavenna

Bellinzona

Adda

L.Como

Lecco

Como

L.Iseo

Oglio

MILAN

Lodi

Marignano

Crema

Cremona

Placenza

Pavia

Bongionno

Melegnano

Lambro

Stradella

Tortona

Voghera

Novara

Vercelli

Mortara

Casale

Alessandria

Acqui

Dego

Marengo

San Giuliano

Montenotte

Spezia

SardiniaNN

TURIN

Pinerolo

Biella

Dora Baltea

Casale

Alba

Cherasco

Carru

Mondovi

Cuneo

Col di Tenda

Pass of Tenda

Oneglia

Ventimiglia

Nizza

Maritime Alps

Tanaro

Stura

Tinea

FLORENCE

Leghorn

LEONAUR
ALSO FROM LEONAUR
AVAILABLE IN SOFTCOVER OR HARDCOVER WITH DUST JACKET

LIFE IN THE ARMY OF NORTHERN VIRGINIA *by Carlton McCarthy*—
The Observations of a Confederate Artilleryman of Cutshaw's Battalion During the
American Civil War 1861-1865.

HISTORY OF THE CAVALRY OF THE ARMY OF THE POTOMAC *by
Charles D. Rhodes*—Including Pope's Army of Virginia and the Cavalry Operations in West Virginia During the American Civil War.

CAMP-FIRE AND COTTON-FIELD *by Thomas W. Knox*—A New York Her-
ald Correspondent's View of the American Civil War.

SERGEANT STILLWELL *by Leander Stillwell* —The Experiences of a Union
Army Soldier of the 61st Illinois Infantry During the American Civil War.

STONEWALL'S CANNONEER *by Edward A. Moore*—Experiences with the
Rockbridge Artillery, Confederate Army of Northern Virginia, During the American
Civil War.

THE SIXTH CORPS *by George Stevens*—The Army of the Potomac, Union
Army, During the American Civil War.

THE RAILROAD RAIDERS *by William Pittenger*—An Ohio Volunteers Recollections of the Andrews Raid to Disrupt the Confederate Railroad in Georgia During the American Civil War.

CITIZEN SOLDIER *by John Beatty*—An Account of the American Civil War by a
Union Infantry Officer of Ohio Volunteers Who Became a Brigadier General.

COX: PERSONAL RECOLLECTIONS OF THE CIVIL WAR--VOLUME 1 *by
Jacob Dolson Cox*—West Virginia, Kanawha Valley, Gauley Bridge, Cotton Mountain, South Mountain, Antietam, the Morgan Raid & the East Tennessee Campaign.

COX: PERSONAL RECOLLECTIONS OF THE CIVIL WAR--VOLUME 2
by Jacob Dolson Cox—Siege of Knoxville, East Tennessee, Atlanta Campaign, the
Nashville Campaign & the North Carolina Campaign.

KERSHAW'S BRIGADE VOLUME 1 *by D. Augustus Dickert*—Manassas, Sev-
en Pines, Sharpsburg (Antietam), Fredricksburg, Chancellorsville, Gettysburg, Chick-
amauga, Chattanooga, Fort Sanders & Bean Station.

KERSHAW'S BRIGADE VOLUME 2 *by D. Augustus Dickert*—At the wilder-
ness, Cold Harbour, Petersburg, The Shenandoah Valley and Cedar Creek..

LEONAUR

ALSO FROM LEONAUR
AVAILABLE IN SOFTCOVER OR HARDCOVER WITH DUST JACKET

THE RELUCTANT REBEL *by William G. Stevenson*—A young Kentuckian's experiences in the Confederate Infantry & Cavalry during the American Civil War..

BOOTS AND SADDLES *by Elizabeth B. Custer*—The experiences of General Custer's Wife on the Western Plains.

FANNIE BEERS' CIVIL WAR *by Fannie A. Beers*—A Confederate Lady's Experiences of Nursing During the Campaigns & Battles of the American Civil War.

LADY SALE'S AFGHANISTAN *by Florentia Sale*—An Indomitable Victorian Lady's Account of the Retreat from Kabul During the First Afghan War.

THE TWO WARS OF MRS DUBERLY *by Frances Isabella Duberly*—An Intrepid Victorian Lady's Experience of the Crimea and Indian Mutiny.

THE REBELLIOUS DUCHESS *by Paul F. S. Dermoncourt*—The Adventures of the Duchess of Berri and Her Attempt to Overthrow French Monarchy.

LADIES OF WATERLOO *by Charlotte A. Eaton, Magdalene de Lancey & Juana Smith*—The Experiences of Three Women During the Campaign of 1815: Waterloo Days by Charlotte A. Eaton, A Week at Waterloo by Magdalene de Lancey & Juana's Story by Juana Smith.

TWO YEARS BEFORE THE MAST *by Richard Henry Dana. Jr.*—The account of one young man's experiences serving on board a sailing brig—the Penelope—bound for California, between the years1834-36.

A SAILOR OF KING GEORGE *by Frederick Hoffman*—From Midshipman to Captain—Recollections of War at Sea in the Napoleonic Age 1793-1815.

LORDS OF THE SEA *by A. T. Mahan*—Great Captains of the Royal Navy During the Age of Sail.

COGGESHALL'S VOYAGES: VOLUME 1 *by George Coggeshall*—The Recollections of an American Schooner Captain.

COGGESHALL'S VOYAGES: VOLUME 2 *by George Coggeshall*—The Recollections of an American Schooner Captain.

TWILIGHT OF EMPIRE *by Sir Thomas Ussher & Sir George Cockburn*—Two accounts of Napoleon's Journeys in Exile to Elba and St. Helena: Narrative of Events by Sir Thomas Ussher & Napoleon's Last Voyage: Extract of a diary by Sir George Cockburn.

LEONAUR

ALSO FROM LEONAUR
AVAILABLE IN SOFTCOVER OR HARDCOVER WITH DUST JACKET

FARAWAY CAMPAIGN *by F. James*—Experiences of an Indian Army Cavalry Officer in Persia & Russia During the Great War.

REVOLT IN THE DESERT *by T. E. Lawrence*—An account of the experiences of one remarkable British officer's war from his own perspective.

MACHINE-GUN SQUADRON *by A. M. G.*—The 20th Machine Gunners from British Yeomanry Regiments in the Middle East Campaign of the First World War.

A GUNNER'S CRUSADE *by Antony Bluett*—The Campaign in the Desert, Palestine & Syria as Experienced by the Honourable Artillery Company During the Great War .

DESPATCH RIDER *by W. H. L. Watson*—The Experiences of a British Army Motorcycle Despatch Rider During the Opening Battles of the Great War in Europe.

TIGERS ALONG THE TIGRIS *by E. J. Thompson*—The Leicestershire Regiment in Mesopotamia During the First World War.

HEARTS & DRAGONS *by Charles R. M. F. Crutwell*—The 4th Royal Berkshire Regiment in France and Italy During the Great War, 1914-1918.

INFANTRY BRIGADE: 1914 *by John Ward*—The Diary of a Commander of the 15th Infantry Brigade, 5th Division, British Army, During the Retreat from Mons.

DOING OUR 'BIT' *by Ian Hay*—Two Classic Accounts of the Men of Kitchener's 'New Army' During the Great War including *The First 100,000* & *All In It*.

AN EYE IN THE STORM *by Arthur Ruhl*—An American War Correspondent's Experiences of the First World War from the Western Front to Gallipoli-and Beyond.

STAND & FALL *by Joe Cassells*—With the Middlesex Regiment Against the Bolsheviks 1918-19.

RIFLEMAN MACGILL'S WAR *by Patrick MacGill*—A Soldier of the London Irish During the Great War in Europe including *The Amateur Army*, *The Red Horizon* & *The Great Push*.

WITH THE GUNS *by C. A. Rose & Hugh Dalton*—Two First Hand Accounts of British Gunners at War in Europe During World War 1- Three Years in France with the Guns and With the British Guns in Italy.

THE BUSH WAR DOCTOR *by Robert V. Dolbey*—The Experiences of a British Army Doctor During the East African Campaign of the First World War.

www.ingramcontent.com/pod-product-compliance
Lightning Source LLC
Chambersburg PA
CBHW032017090426

42741CB00006B/625